THE SOURCES OF HISTORY:
STUDIES IN THE USES OF HISTORICAL EVIDENCE

GENERAL EDITOR: G. R. ELTON

The Sources of History:
Studies in the Uses of Historical Evidence

Great Britain Since 1914

by
C. L. MOWAT

CORNELL UNIVERSITY PRESS
Ithaca, New York

First published 1971

International Standard Book Number 0-8014-0632-3
Library of Congress Catalog Card Number 79-147277
Printed in Great Britain

Contents

General Editor's Introduction

By what right do historians claim that their reconstructions of the past are true, or at least on the road to truth? How much of the past can they hope to recover: are there areas that will remain for ever dark, questions that will never receive an answer? These are problems which should and do engage not only the scholar and student but every serious reader of history. In the debates on the nature of history, however, attention commonly concentrates on philosophic doubts about the nature of historical knowledge and explanation, or on the progress that might be made by adopting supposedly new methods of analysis. The disputants hardly ever turn to consider the materials with which historians work and which must always lie at the foundation of their structures. Yet, whatever theories or methods the scholar may embrace, unless he knows his sources and rests upon them he will not deserve the name of historian. The bulk of historical evidence is much larger and more complex than most laymen and some professions seem to know, and a proper acquaintance with it tends to prove both exhilarating and sobering—exhilarating because it opens the road to unending enquiry, and sobering because it reduces the inspiring theory and the new method to their proper subordinate place in the scheme of things. It is the purpose of this series to bring this fact to notice by showing what we have and how it may be used.

G. R. ELTON

In Memoriam

Charles Loch Mowat was born at Oxford on 4 October 1913; he died at Bangor, much too soon, on 23 June 1970. The son of the historian R. B. Mowat, he was himself a professional historian and teacher of history to his fingertips. At one time he appeared to have decided to make the United States his permanent home, but after a highly successful career at the Universities of Minnesota (1934–6), California (1936–50) and Chicago (1950–8) he returned to Britain, to become Professor of History at the University College of North Wales at Bangor, a post he held to his death. His interests concentrated on the most recent period of British history; the book that made him famous was *Britain between the Wars* (1955), still easily the most balanced and perceptive survey of the theme. When the Cambridge University Press discovered that the original version of the last volume of the *New Cambridge Modern History* had been commissioned too early and needed replacing, Mowat was the obvious man to approach, and he discharged his very difficult task with his accustomed brilliance, efficiency and speed (1961). Characteristically also he did it without causing the slightest friction or upsetting a single person—to anyone familiar with this kind of work a fantastic achievement.

There are few men like Charles Mowat, and the large circle of his friends will miss him to the end of their days. Worse still, his going is a shattering loss to the difficult area of history which he had made his own. Contemporary history is always fuller of problems than any other; it badly needed his knowledge, sanity, sense, and awareness of the need to reflect upon the methods which could render the accumulating mass of materials manageable and produce enduring understanding of matters in which the historian is himself bound to be involved. It is thus some small consolation that he has left us this book. With the fortitude so characteristic of him, he completed it under great difficulties during his last illness, a deed of quiet heroism. There were a few details to which he still wished to attend—a small correction here, a minor elaboration there. I had discussed the book with him throughout, and I have done what was necessary to carry out his wishes. Charles Mowat the friend and the historian is dead; Charles Mowat the teacher lives on in these pages, a shrewd, learned and inspiring helper to future generations of scholars.

G. R. E.

CHAPTER 1

Since 1914: Recent or Contemporary?

Historians must be able to produce sound and trustworthy history even in circumstances which do not permit them to see everything; there should be rules of scholarship applicable . . . to ensure that even a partial view of the evidence avoids the uncertainties of personal selection.

It is one of the shortcomings of more recent history that its practitioners, overwhelmed by the task of mere study, have done almost nothing so far to work out proper rules of this kind.[1]

To the historian of recent times this challenge from the editor of this series may seem an irrelevance; or it may stir him to ask some fundamental questions about his work and his evidence. How does he know that his account of recent British history is a faithful portrayal of the times? What is his evidence? What of the mass of evidence which inevitably, being mortal, he has not used? What things which now seem or perhaps only in the future will seem important has he omitted, and what topics has he over-emphasised? The answers to these questions may emerge in what follows; but before getting down to cases it will be well to suggest other approaches and difficulties in the way of recent history.

Let us approach the history of Great Britain since 1914 with another set of questions. Suppose you are setting out to write a history of some part of this period, or of the whole of the last fifty or sixty years, or of some limited subject within the period, how will you start? What books will you go to first? What sources are there, as opposed to other people's accounts or impressions? How far can the value of the sources be tested? Or suppose you are a reader, and wish to read about the General Strike of 1926, or the period of 'appeasement', the blitz of London in 1940 or the post-

[1] G. R. Elton, *The Practice of History* (London, 1967), 89–90.

war 'age of austerity', the Suez crisis of 1956 or the history of Harold Wilson's government, how far can you accept what you read? Is the book accurate, impartial, balanced? What are its sources?

The answer will depend on the subject and the book, but also on the author and the reader. Recent history, by which I mean history which is within the living memory of at least the older generation, means different things to readers of different ages. To the older reader it is part of his own private history; he lived through much or all of it, and he has his own personal memories (hazy or distorted or limited though they may be) by which to check the authenticity of what he reads. 'It wasn't like that at all', or 'I'd quite forgotten that', or 'I don't remember anything of that' may be his comments. On the other hand, to the younger man or woman the war of 1914–18 or the depression of the thirties, or the Second World War or the time of Harold Macmillan may be as remote as Egypt under the Pharaohs or the England of Elizabeth I. When does personal history start? One might say, for the sake of argument, around the age of twelve. Before that one remembers little about the national or world scene; childhood memories of school and holidays, brothers and sisters and friends, parents and aunts and uncles hold sway. After twelve one's private memories become mixed with a more public memory of the times; we may not be able to put a date, even a year, to a particular event, but we remember it as news. The credibility of recent history, therefore, depends more than the history of earlier times on the experience of the reader himself; his experience may give him much guidance, or little, in accepting or questioning what he reads. The same thing applies with greater or less force to the potential writer of recent history; personal experience and memory may put him on the track of research, or he may have to depend on the advice and writings of older men.

There is, however, another distinction to be made in our subject: it is really two, recent and contemporary history. Contemporary history is a term which is now much used, but with little precision as to its meaning. The Association of Contemporary

Historians, founded in 1967, has taken the twentieth century for its domain. Other historians would take it back into the nineteenth century, as several articles in the *Journal of Contemporary History* (founded in 1966) have done. All these usages seem unjustifiable. The history of the First World War, between the wars, even the 1950s, is not contemporary to a great many people, as we have already seen. 1900 is seventy years ago, as far back as 1830, the time of the great Reform Bill, was to the man or woman of the year 1900. Moreover, as the twentieth century advances, the contemporaneity of its earlier years become even more remote. One can even quibble and say that no history can be contemporary: the present moment has passed as soon as we have lived it.

There is another meaning applied to contemporary history, one which has been developed with great force and persuasiveness by Geoffrey Barraclough. Contemporary history, to him, is a new age in history, following the end of 'modern history'. Its essential character is that it is world history: no part of the world is now unaffected by events anywhere else. 'One of the distinctive facts about contemporary history is that it is world history and that the forces shaping it cannot be understood unless we are prepared to adopt world-wide perspectives.'[1] When this new age began is open to debate; perhaps the whole period from 1895 to 1955 is the period of transition from modern to contemporary. Its marks are the dwarfing of Europe, the rise of the super-powers (Russia, the United States, China), the resurgence of new nation states in Africa and Asia following the end of the European empires, the threat of wars and civil wars between white and coloured peoples, the ever more rapid development and extension of industry and technology, the advances of science, including the exploration of space, the revolutionary discoveries in genetics and biology, the population explosion, the possibility of man's self-annihilation or self-poisoning, and the new moods of political revolution spreading from Maoist China or from Castro's Cuba, particularly among university students in almost every country. The list could

[1] G. Barraclough, *An Introduction to Contemporary History* (London, 1964), 2–4.

easily be prolonged; in particular one might add the ever-accelerating rate of change in the world.[1]

It is not, however, contemporary history in this sense with which we are here concerned, except indirectly. It is, rather, with that part of British history which can be called contemporary. Here, again, dating can be arbitrary. We might say that contemporary history begins at the point at which government records remain closed, which at present is thirty years; before that we are in the realm of recent history. Since each year's papers are opened thirty years later, this would give us a shifting date, 1940 at the time of publication of this book, 1941 the year following, and so forth. This is a clue to the starting-point of contemporary history, but it is hardly decisive. What matters is how much has been written about a particular time in an authoritative way, based on a variety of sources, even though without the benefit of government archives. It is a question of what has 'passed into history' in the sense of there being a generally agreed and fairly widespread view of the time. By this test the Second World War and the post-war Labour government of Clement Attlee (1945-51) belong to recent history; how much of the 1950s and 1960s—a period of almost twenty years—should still be called 'contemporary' is debatable. Contemporary history's essence is its open-endedness. Like the Mississippi, it rolls on without cease.

Hence in strictly contemporary history one begins by being completely at sea—in fact, worse than that, for at sea one should have adequate charts and tables. The subject is undefined. No historian has yet written about the period, selecting events, constructing a framework which his rivals and successors must either follow or controvert. All other historians, consciously or not, stand on their predecessors' shoulders; the contemporary historian must stand on his own feet. He must decide what to include, what to emphasise, without the benefit of documents or memoirs

[1] In addition to Barraclough's *Introduction*, see his article, 'Universal History', in H. P. R. Finberg (ed.), *Approaches to History* (London, 1962). Cf. C. L. Mowat, Ch. 1, 'Introductory survey: on the limits of modern history', *New Cambridge Modern History*, Vol. XII, 2nd edition, *The Shifting Balance of World Forces* (Cambridge, 1968).

or any agreed account. He must go by his own memory of the years, reinforced by the reading of newspapers and periodicals, contemporary books discussing political, economic and social problems, reports of scientific advances and of technological innovations. His choice of material, more than that of other historians, will be highly personal, governed partly not by what seemed important two or three years ago but by what seems important now and which he thinks may be important in future years. Thus his account can only be provisional, a piece of historical journalism—and if it achieves that level it will have served its purpose well. For it is the journalist and the commentator who will, in one medium or another, be his principal source. And his first ally will be the editor and compiler; those who write annual reviews for newspapers or encyclopaedias or year books, and the authors of the *Annual Register*. The stored memories of computers will in future become more important for him.

We may, however, be exaggerating the contemporary historian's difficulties. The problems of 'sources', authenticity, accuracy, judgment which he faces are not very different from any other historian's. What he lacks are the memoirs and diaries which will later fill out, or perhaps distort, the narrative, and the use of the government's records. And these at best take time to get incorporated into the history of the period, and when they do are more likely to alter points of detail than the main outlines. What he chiefly lacks is perspective.

Recent history, at any rate—history from 1914 to whatever point the shifting line of acceptance has reached—is really conventional history, when it comes to its sources and standards. Writer and reader may be under some handicaps as compared to the historian of Victorian England; they may also have certain advantages. The sources of both are largely the same, and much that is said in the volume in this series for the period 1800–1914 applies equally to recent British history. The problem of selection, given the enormous mass of material evidence of all sorts surviving from the Victorian age and from the first half of the twentieth century, is similar.

Similar also are the choices about the scope and kinds of recent history which may be written. Those historians who so far have written about the period on any considerable scale have attempted to give a narrative of the traditional sort, using the political history (including foreign policy and war) as the frame and working in economic and social history as the narrative proceeds. A. J. P. Taylor's *English History 1914–1945* (Oxford, 1965), W. N. Medlicott's *Contemporary England, 1914–1964* (London, 1967), A. F. Havighurst's *Twentieth-Century Britain* (New York, 1962) and my *Britain between the Wars, 1918–1940* (London, 1955, paperback edition, 1968) follow this plan. Arthur Marwick's *Britain in the Century of Total War* (London, 1968) is more analytical in its attempt to assess the effects of the two wars, and inevitably brings together political, economic and social forces. On the other hand, *The Deluge* (London, 1965) by the same author is a history of the First World War, as experienced in Britain, with the political and military sides left out. No one has attempted an over-all history of that war, though Paul Guinn, in *British Strategy and Politics 1914–1918* (Oxford, 1965) has made a pioneering study of the inter-action of politics and military strategy. Both wars have had their military and naval history written in official volumes. For both there is also a notable series of books on the economic and industrial aspects, including studies of manpower and labour, agriculture, shipping and land transport, economic blockade, rationing and government controls.[1]

In fact, historians of recent Britain have in general followed traditional lines. There have been valuable economic histories,[2] many diplomatic studies,[3] a few rather light-hearted surveys[4] of

[1] See below, Ch. 7, pp. 184–6.

[2] A. J. Youngson, *Britain's Economic Growth 1920–1966* (London, 1967); S. Pollard, *The Development of the British Economy 1914–1954* (London, 1962).

[3] See F. S. Northedge, *The Troubled Giant: Britain among the Great Powers 1916–1963* (London, 1966), and W. N. Medlicott, *British Foreign Policy since Versailles, 1919–1963* (London, 1968) for guidance.

[4] R. Graves and A. Hodge, *The Long Week-End: A Social History of Great Britain 1918–1939* (London, 1940; paperback, 1965); R. Blythe, *The Age of Illusion: England in the Twenties and Thirties* (London, 1963).

social history. Books relating the literature and art of the time to its general history have been rare; Julian Symons attempted it, partly autobiographically, in *The Thirties: A Dream Revolved* (London, 1960). Military histories of the inter-war years have only recently begun to appear.[1] The history of science, at least for the layman, remains almost unwritten. The dangers of this sort of separation are more easily seen than avoided. The problems raised by the different kinds of histories are indeed serious, and will be treated in a later chapter.

[1] Robin Higham, *Armed Forces in Peacetime: Britain 1918–1940, a case study* (Hamden, Connecticut, 1962); S. W. Roskill, *Naval Policy between the Wars*, Vol. I, *1919–1929* (London, 1968).

CHAPTER 2

Standard and Official

I. WORKS OF REFERENCE

Works of reference may seem at the farthest remove from sources. One thinks at once of the reference section of a busy public library, with rows of heavy volumes on the shelves and helpful—if far too little valued—assistants at the desk. An expert reference librarian must be today's equivalent of the old polymath scholar; he must have at his fingertips the title and place of a hundred and one different books to which to refer the endless enquirers with their multifarious questions, and if he cannot answer a question immediately he must know where to look for the answer. Indeed, guides to reference works are themselves volumes of considerable size,[1] though in future they and many of the books they lead to may be replaced (indeed in some medical and scientific subjects are already being replaced) by information-retrieval systems by which the enquirer is connected to the data bank of a central computer and can be given a print-out slip listing references to articles and books bearing on the subject of his enquiry.

A moment's thought will show not only that this is the way in which most courses of reading or study must begin (one goes to an encyclopaedia or work of reference or asks someone what books to begin with), but also that the reference works are themselves sources. It needs no demonstration that an out-of-date city or county directory, for example an old *Kelly's Directory*, is a prime source for topography, for streets and houses, for the residents of a town and the principal occupations of its inhabitants a century or half a century ago, and that a series of such directories will show

[1] A. J. Walford, *Guide to Reference Material* (London, 1959); R. L. Collison, *Bibliographies, Subject and National: a guide to their contents* . . . 3rd ed. (London, 1968).

23

the economic and social changes taking place over a number of years. For recent history, reference works are equally sources: past volumes of *Whitaker's Almanack* are already historical works, and more recent volumes may be the only accessible source for particulars of institutions, officials, salaries, trade, local government, population—indeed, almost anything. The *Statesman's Year Book* serves a similar purpose, chiefly on the governmental side, and with a coverage much larger than *Whitaker's* on all the countries of the world. In a different category, but only because it is official, is the *Annual Abstract of Statistics* made up from the *Monthly Digest of Statistics*. These two series have, since 1946, replaced the Board of Trade's great series, the *Statistical Abstract for the United Kingdom*. Here will be found tables of trade, production, finance, population, housing, social services, health, crime, education, employment and unemployment, occupation, mining, manufacturing, agriculture, transport, banking, prices, national income and expenditure.

Guides to what was news but is soon history are equally indispensable, particularly for contemporary history. Is a newspaper a source for an account of a particular event or series of events and their causes, or is it simply useful as a record of what people were told at the time, what they and the reporters thought had happened, what was current opinion of current events and issues? We shall have to consider newspapers as sources later. The immediate question is how to consult them. For they are not easy to handle. The monthly bound volumes of a daily paper (or the semi-annual volumes of a local weekly paper) are of great weight and need a large table or sloping desk if they are to be used at all. If the newspaper is preserved on film it is only slightly more easy to manipulate, and the eye-strain in reading it may be greater; one will have to run many feet of film backwards and forwards to find the pages or columns one wants. In fact newspapers are virtually unusable, or at least entail much weariness of the flesh, if one is simply to go through a file or volume, day by day and week by week. There are, however, two short cuts. There is *The Times Index*, published bi-monthly, from which one can establish the dates of events and the relative importance of contemporary issues and ideas, and one can use this knowledge in consulting any other newspaper, even though it is not indexed, or a periodical (a weekly or a monthly) which probably has an index. Or one may use *Keesing's Contemporary Archives*, which began in 1931. This gives digests of the news almost day by day, and has a very full set of cumulative indexes.

Biographical information can also be got from works of reference, but it is likely to be disappointing. *Who's Who* contains entries for a very large but somewhat arbitrary range of eminent and not-so-eminent men and women. Certain categories of people, those with titles, holders of public offices, members of parliament, the higher military and naval officers and clergy, judges and other members of the establishment, including a certain number of professors, are to be found in its pages (or, correspondingly, in the useful ten-year volumes, *Who was Who*, containing the final entries of those who have died within the period). But if you want to find out something about an engineer or an architect, an author or artist, who is untitled or in other ways not yet recognised, a scientist or a businessman who has not become accepted as a public figure, you will not find him—still less her—in its many pages. On the other hand, if the person you seek is included, how reliable is the information, which is supplied by the subject himself? Wives disappear, embarrassing earlier ventures are omitted from later entries. At best you find only names of parents and wives or husbands, bare details of education, career, offices, honours, books, recreations.

The decennial supplements of the *Dictionary of National Biography* are also open to criticism. The latest volume published to date includes those people who died in 1941–50. It is not so much the time-lag between career or death (which may follow long years of inactive retirement) and appearance in the *D.N.B.* which matters: a collaborative volume of this sort cannot be written quickly, and there is always a small minority of laggard contributors to hold up the whole work. Nor is the question of exclusion so serious. Any capable reviewer can play the game of pointing

out important people who should have been included and were
not; he might even ask the opposite question, why some people
were there, and posit a law of inverse eminence: the rarer the
specialism, the more abstruse the scholar, the more mandarin the
civil servant, the more likely he is to make the grade. The choice
of those to include is made only after a very careful scrutiny of
long lists of people in many categories; it is in no way haphazard.
The difficulty about the *D.N.B.* as a source is that, in the bulk of
the entries (of half a page to a page), little can be said about the
man beyond the facts of his career. The references given are often
no more than obituaries and two mystic sources, 'private information' and 'personal knowledge'. On the other hand, this does
illustrate the value of the *D.N.B.* as a source: it can use the information of living people which would otherwise be lost. This can
be especially useful for preserving something of the personality of
the man, and is apparent in several of the longer articles.[1]

Last but not least is the *Annual Register*, which since 1947 has
been edited with the help of a committee representing the Royal
Institute of International Affairs and other learned bodies; its title
is now the *Annual Register of World Events*. This contains chapters
chronicling the year's events month by month for Great Britain,
followed by chapters on the year's history in different countries
and the main events in religion, trade and finance, science and the
arts and literature. This can hardly be regarded as a source except
that as time goes on it mirrors what people, or at least the editor
and contributors, thought was important at the time, whether in
happenings or the realm of ideas. The latest volumes are instant,
or not so instant, history, and they are invaluable to anyone
setting out on the sea of contemporary history. They provide the
first provisional charts, the first frame of reference.

2. GOVERNMENT REPORTS

The manifold publications of the government must be regarded as
a main source, but they are not equally usable and accessible. The

[1] For an analysis of the *D.N.B.*, 1941–50, see my review in *History*, XLV,
190–3 (June, 1960).

main series is the *Parliamentary Papers*, which are bound up each
year into a set of some thirty or more large volumes. There is an
index volume from which one can usually find the volume and
place in which a particular paper is bound. The series includes all
papers ordered by or laid before either House of Parliament and
papers printed by Command of the government and given a
Cmd. or Cmnd. number. *Parliamentary Papers* thus include parliamentary bills, estimates and accounts, treaties and other papers on
foreign policy, reports of government departments (e.g. annual
reports of the Board of Education and its successors) and reports of
parliamentary committees and royal commissions. Particulars can
be found in the annual *Catalogue of Government Publications*
(formerly the *Consolidated List of Government Publications*) published by H.M. Stationery Office. Professor and Mrs Ford (P. & G.
Ford) have published an invaluable series of guides and breviates.
Their *Breviate of Parliamentary Papers, 1917-1939* (Oxford, 1951)
and *1940-1954* (Oxford, 1961) not only provide a list of papers
and reports arranged by subject-matter, but give abstracts of their
contents. Their *Guide to Parliamentary Papers* (Oxford, 1955) is an
admirable brief introduction whose contents are summarised in
the sub-title: *What they are: How to find them: How to use them.* It
renders any further exposition of the subject superfluous. It
should perhaps be noted that the old term 'Blue Book' for a
government report is really an anachronism today, when reports
are published in covers of different colours and sometimes with
some eye-appeal. 'White Paper' is perhaps still appropriate for
many shorter documents.

A large part of the government's official publications will not be
found in the *Parliamentary Papers*. They are non-command papers,
and for the historian are often more important than the Command
papers. They include reports of departmental committees and
working parties, of the boards of nationalised industries (including
such documents as the Beeching Report on the *Reshaping of
British Railways* (London, 1963), and the minutes of evidence of
royal commissions and committees whose actual reports are in the
Command series. All are listed in the Stationery Office's monthly

and annual catalogue. For most users it may not matter whether a paper is in *Parliamentary Papers* or not, since only the largest libraries will have the series. Smaller libraries should, however, possess important government reports and papers, whether parliamentary or non-parliamentary, and they will be catalogued under their individual titles (not, usually, under the name of the committee's chairman, which is the usual 'shorthand' way of referring to a report).

Of the materials in both categories, the Reports of Royal Commissions and other committees appointed to go into particular questions have always attracted the historian's special attention. They may perhaps be put into two main groups. There are committees which the government appoints to deal with some urgent matter, and there are those entrusted with the task of thinking about some long-range problem. Either kind of committee may produce one of two results: it may help to settle policy and lead directly to action, or it may simply produce a report (years later historians may discern the seeds of policy in its labours). The reason for appointing the first type of committee may be partly to buy time, to take the heat out of an issue, to avoid an immediate crisis by delay and postponement. Examples include the two great enquiries into the coalmining industry after the First World War.

The Coal Industry Commission of 1919, always called the Sankey Commission from its chairman, Sir John Sankey, was created (unusually, by an act of parliament) by Lloyd George's Coalition government as an answer to the miners' threat of a national coal strike if their demands for a six-hour day, a thirty per cent increase in wages and the nationalisation of the mines were not immediately conceded, while the mines were still under the government's wartime control. The Commission consisted of the chairman, a judge, and twelve other members, six representing the men's side of the dispute and six the owners and business. The former group consisted of the three chief officers of the Miners' Federation and three economists friendly to Labour, R. H. Tawney, Sidney Webb and Sir Leo Chiozza Money. The latter group comprised three coalminers and three industrialists not

connected with the industry. It presented a number of reports.
Three were on the question of hours and wages and represented
the miners' and owners' positions and a middle ground taken by
Sankey and the industrialists; the last was, needless to say, accepted
by the government, and ultimately by all concerned. On the
question of nationalisation the committee presented four reports:
against (the owners and two industrialists), for (the miners and
economists and, in a separate report, Sankey) and a compromise,
the grouping of collieries under district boards which would
operate as private companies but under certain controls, the proposal of the remaining member, Sir Arthur Duckham. This
division of opinion enabled the government to avoid any positive
decision. It claimed that there was no clear verdict for nationalisation, which to the miner was a complete betrayal of their trust and
of the promises, as they believed, which had been made to them
when the Commission was appointed; they pointed to a seven to
six majority of the members in favour of nationalisation. The
government, however, offered only the Duckham plan, and
when both sides rejected it, did nothing. The mines were later
decontrolled and returned to private ownership. But long before
this the government's tactic had taken the heat out of the nationalisation issue; during the Commission's hearings the public had
lost interest and the miners the sympathy of the trade union
movement: and the miners themselves, having won much of
their demands over wages and hours, were less ready to fight over
the ownership of the mines.

The Sankey commission is a classic among such bodies. Its
reports propound alternative policies. They contain information,
historical, descriptive, statistical, about the coal industry. And the
minutes of evidence, which somewhat unusually were published
with the reports and not as separate volumes, give the verbatim
text of the Commission's examination of witnesses day by day.
The miners and their allies used the commission to put on the
stand and cross-examine the mine owners and the royalty owners.
The latter were asked to justify the large sums they drew in
royalties from the miners' toil. The managerial efficiency of the

owners was challenged. Miners' wives were brought up to London to testify to the miserable condition of the houses they were forced to live in. The Commission's sessions in the King's Robing Room in the House of Lords made good copy at the time and make lively reading today. Here are two passages from the evidence of the Duke of Northumberland:

> 15,160 [Herbert Smith]. Is it not worth your while to see how these people live, to see what causes these deaths [infant mortality]?—You think landowners have nothing to do but examine statistics. I am a hard-worked man. I am not a privileged man like you. I cannot afford to waste time sitting on a commission like this.
> 15,161. I think you do nothing at all?—That is where you are wrong.

> 15,182 [Sir Leo Money]. Would you kindly tell us what particular service it is you perform to the community *qua* coal owner.—I really do not quite know what you mean, *qua* coal owner.
> 15,183. Exactly what I say.—I do not know what you mean.
> 15,184. As a coal owner what service do you perform to the community? —As the owner of coal I do not think I perform any service to the community—not as owner of the coal.[1]

But how valuable are the Sankey Commission's volumes to the historian? The Commission was a historical event, and it influenced other events: the inaction of the government, the acquiescence of the miners. It did not, except perhaps over wages and hours, lead directly to decisions of policy. The factual information it contains is valuable, but some of it could be got from other government documents or from trade and professional journals. Its members were men of strong character and feeling; their opinions, and hence their advice, were bound to be subjective. The fact that a statement appears in a committee's report or in minutes of evidence is no guarantee that it is true. This source, in other words, must be used with all the caution which the historian

[1] Coal Industry Commission, Vol. II, *Reports and Minutes of Evidence on the Second Stage of the Inquiry* (Cmd. 360: 1919), *Parliamentary Papers*, 1919, Vol. XII.

applies to any other source: he must know the context, the personalities, he must apply all the usual tests to which he subjects historical evidence, he must check information from this source against that which other sources provide.

The next major report on the coalmines, the Samuel Report, is quite different. In the summer of 1925, when another coal strike, and even a general strike in support of it, was threatened, the Conservative government of Stanley Baldwin set up the Royal Commission on the Coal Industry (1925). This consisted of three men of affairs unconnected with the industry, Sir William Beveridge, the economist, a banker and a cotton manufacturer, and the chairman, Sir Herbert Samuel, a Liberal politician who at the time was neither in office or parliament, having recently been High Commissioner in Palestine. Again, evidence was heard and papers were submitted: these are to be found in three separate volumes. The Report itself is two things in one. It is a full and critical analysis of the industry, bringing out the decline in production and exports, the paucity of research, the limited degree of mechanisation, the disparity between the different coalfields and between large and small mines, the heterogeneity within the industry, in which competing ownership of the coal and the mines meant much inefficiency (seams could be more effectively mined if separate ownership did not prevent linking up mines underground). It is also a series of proposals, which one might call personal judgments. It rejects nationalisation. It favours some rather undefined reorganisation. It rejects longer hours but declares for a reduction of wages: 'a disaster is impending over the industry, and the immediate reduction in working costs that can be effected in this way, and in this way alone, is essential to save it.' This was a unanimous report. It attempted to hold the balance between the two sides. It strongly criticises the owners for refusing to meet the miners for national discussions (as opposed to district negotiations) and for charging the miners with deliberate restriction of production and attempts to destroy the industry's prosperity in order to compel its nationalisation. It is equally critical of the miners for their charges of failures in the management of the mines.

The result was, of course, rejection of the Report by both sides. The men would not accept lower wages; the owners were insulted by the advice to reorganise their industry. The government used the disagreement as an excuse to do nothing. The coal strike of 1926 and the General Strike of May 4 to 12 followed, and the miners were ultimately defeated. The Report, therefore, produced delay and inaction (or action by doing nothing); it summarised a large amount of information not easily to be found elsewhere. If we divide committee reports into those which frame policy and those which do not, the Samuel Report falls into the second class (except in so far as inaction is a policy).

Another committee appointed to gain time in a developing crisis, but one which helped to decide policy, was the Committee on National Expenditure appointed by Philip Snowden, the Labour Chancellor of the Exchequer, early in 1931 when a budgetary deficit seemed to threaten. This, like the earlier similarly named committee of 1922 better known from its chairman as the Geddes Committee, was a committee to examine national expenditure and propose economies. Its chairman was Sir George May, recently secretary of the Prudential Assurance Company; its other members were businessmen and two Labour M.P.s. Its majority report helped to bring about the political crisis of August 1931 in which the Labour government fell. For it produced, on the basis of evidence provided by the Treasury, an alarming report of a large impending deficit and recommended severe economies including a twenty per cent cut in payments to the unemployed. In fact it probably exaggerated the budgetary position, and its recommendations only embraced a limited range of expedients. But its text provided confirmation for fears, both at home and abroad, about the country's financial health: a flight from the pound and the political crisis followed. The new National government carried out the spirit of the Report by increasing taxes and making cuts of ten per cent in salaries and wages to government employees and to the unemployed. The dissenting report of the two Labour members of the committee was completely ignored. What are we to make of the majority report as a historical source?

The Report itself was a fact, a happening; the information it contains is a mixture of facts, supposed facts and contemporary inferences from facts and suppositions, and none of it can be accepted as 'the truth' without further evidence or verification.

Another example of a Report which was the outcome of an emergency was that of the Tribunal under the chairmanship of Sir H. L. Parker, a judge, set up to investigate alleged leakages of information about the rise in the Bank Rate which took place on 19 September 1957. The matter was complicated by the fact that the government was planning new financial measures to meet the recurrence of crisis in the country's trading position; rumours of these measures, announced on the same day (19 September), could have encouraged speculation without anyone having foreknowledge of the rise in the Bank Rate. The Tribunal found, after examining 132 witnesses and considering written statements from 236 other persons, that there had been no prior disclosure. The Report, though brief, is informative, indeed lively, and the minutes of evidence, which were published, are doubtless even more so. The reader learns something of the style of business correspondence, of talk of selling 'Gilts' and delays while directors are grouse-shooting in Scotland, of how Lazard Brothers conduct their business, of the business connections between Directors of the Bank of England; he learns the names of various banking and stockbrokers' firms. A girl of eighteen, a learner typist at the Conservative Central Office, had told her cousin, an older man who was a civil servant, in a crowded train from Woking to Waterloo, that she got much inside information in her job: 'the lot'. She added that they were expecting the police any day about 'this Bank Rate business'. This was dismissed as said in jest. A *Reynolds News* reporter had overheard a conversation between two civil servants (neither Treasury men) at Watford station on 20 September from which he gathered that one of them had had prior knowledge of the rise in Bank Rate. *Reynolds News* used this information on 22 September, saying 'Last night came information that the Cabinet's decision was known to more than one Treasury Official—not of top rank—twenty-four hours before the announcement.' This was put down to loose talk about knowing something of the government's restrictive measures in advance. Finally there was Mrs Dorothy Campbell, who attended a cocktail party at 6.30 pm on Wednesday, 18 September.

> At that party she stated in the presence of Mr. Whitley, Mrs. Gellatly and Mr. Bobby Howes that she had come from the City that afternoon and that she had heard that the Bank Rate was going up the next day by one-and-a-half per cent. Shortly after the increase in the Bank Rate was announced, Mrs. Campbell in a telephone conversation with a Mr. Fitzgibbon claimed prior knowledge of the increase.

'Mrs. Campbell', the Tribunal reported, 'was a most unsatisfactory witness.' However, it was satisfied that she had not been in the City that afternoon and had not been told by anyone of a rise in the Bank Rate, 'but that she made what was intended to be a sensational remark in order to draw attention to herself. Indeed Mr. Fitzgibbon informed us that Mrs. Campbell was in the habit of making remarks of this nature, and from our observation of her we can readily believe it.'[1]

Government reports cover such a wide range of occasions and issues that one or two examples cannot do justice to the class. There are, for example, commissions, or sometimes individual commissioners, appointed to make an enquiry into some matter of urgency. There is then no place for formal hearings or minutes of evidence; the commissioner gathers evidence as best he can, on the spot and by letter or telephone, obtains information from government departments and local authorities, and draws up his report, probably in a matter of weeks rather than months. In 1917 the government created Commissions of Enquiry into Industrial Unrest to look into the causes of trouble on the home front at that stage of the war. Reports were published on eight areas a month

---

[1] *Report of the Tribunal appointed to Inquire into Allegations of Improper Disclosure of Information relating to the Raising of the Bank Rate* (Cmdn. 350: 1958), especially 33–4, 36. The minutes of evidence were published in a separate volume.

Standard and Official

later; their descriptions of bad housing, the impact of high prices,
profiteering, weak beer and restricted licensing hours, were
graphic and compelling.[1] A later example comes from the dis-
tressed areas of heavy unemployment in the early thirties. The
Board of Trade in 1932 published surveys of several areas (Lanca-
shire, Merseyside, the north-east coast, South Wales, South-west
Scotland) which had been conducted by local universities. In 1934
the government appointed four commissioners (two members of
parliament, two businessmen) to investigate conditions in Scotland
and certain depressed areas in England and Wales. Their reports
were published as a Command paper.[2]

Reports of the second type, those dealing with long-range
questions of policy, are numerous and voluminous, particularly
if their minutes of evidence, briefs of interested parties, appendices
and tables are printed. Some lead quite rapidly to decision and
action; of others the seed falls on stony ground, or germinates
only after a long lapse of time. To the historian it makes little
difference. Effective reports will contain a mass of supporting
information and analysis coupled with arguments for proposals
which were eventually embodied in government policy. Ineffective reports may well contain even more bulky information and
equally cogent argument. Both kinds of reports are sources in
themselves, and are also historical facts; and inaction on their
recommendations is as much a decision of government (even if
never formally taken) as action.

Two formidable examples are the reports of two committees
appointed to go into different aspects of the economic stagnation
which seemed to affect the country in the 1920s. The first was the
Balfour Committee, officially the Committee on Industry and
Trade, appointed by the Labour government in 1924 with Sir
Arthur Balfour, a Sheffield steel manufacturer, as chairman. Its
mandate was 'to enquire into the conditions and prospects of

[1] Cited in Arthur Marwick, *The Deluge: British Society and the First World
War* (London, 1965), 205-7.
[2] Ministry of Labour, *Reports of Investigations into the Industrial Conditions in
Certain Depressed Areas* (Cmd. 4728: 1934).

British industry, with special reference to the export trade', and it was asked to look into industrial relations, management, raw materials supplies, the ability of British industry to meet foreign competition, employment and unemployment, and the standard of living. It was at work for five years, producing six reports on particular subjects on the way. These covered overseas markets, industrial relations, industrial efficiency (two reports), the metal industries and the textile industries. These are in the nature of textbooks, a mass of information, description, statistics. The final report (1929) summarised the earlier reports but made no real recommendations. The tone was reassuring. British rates of taxation, for example, were not considered serious handicaps to industry; nor were local rates, customs and tariff policies, transport or labour relations. The rationalisation of industry was to be the path to future progress. A minority of trade union and Labour members of the committee signed a report criticising their colleagues for acceptance of things as they were when under-production and under-consumption were serious hindrances in the home market. They wanted greater public control, the nationalisation of the mines, better education and housing, and doubted whether the necessary reorganisation of industry would ever take place under capitalism. By the time the final report appeared the depression of 1930–4 was already at hand.

The Macmillan Committee under the chairmanship of H. P. Macmillan, a Scottish lawyer, later a lord of appeal, was officially the Committee on Finance and Industry, appointed by Philip Snowden, Labour Chancellor of the Exchequer, in November 1929 at the time when signs of depression were multiplying. Its task was to enquire into 'banking, finance and credit' and to see whether shortcomings in these sectors were handicapping British industry and trade. The Committee was made up of economists and financiers and men of industrial and labour connections; J. M. Keynes and Ernest Bevin were to be its most famous members. Again, the chief result was a textbook on the working of the City of London, the banks, acceptance and discount houses, gold and currency, international investment, monetary policy and prices, the supply of capital. The Report's tone was reassuring; for instance, it claimed that London's short-term borrowing (money, including hot money, accepted from overseas lenders and depositors, and not all covered by liquid or readily available funds and credits) had been declining. Many of its recommendations were technical; one, against devaluing the pound, was positive enough. The Report did not, however, conceal the division of opinion within the Committee. There were several dissenting addenda, particularly one signed by Bevin, Keynes, Reginald McKenna (chairman of the Midland Bank) and three others warning against policies of retrenchment and lower wages and asking for stimulus to industry from replanning, rebuilding and new capital works.

The Macmillan Report's subsequent history was somewhat different from that of the Balfour Report. The Report was published on 13 July 1931, a little over a fortnight before the May Report. The latter got the limelight and helped to precipitate the political crisis. The pound was momentarily saved, only to be devalued by the National government on 21 September. So much for 'Macmillan's' advice. Later historians have turned not so much to the Report as to the minutes of evidence. Here can be seen the confrontation between 'orthodox' economic ideas and the new ideas which Keynes, in particular, was moving towards regarding saving and investment. He was himself, unusually for a member of a committee, a witness for five days (20, 21, 28 February, 6 and 7 March 1930) and expounded his views to his colleagues.[1] Here also are to be found the verbatim reports of two notable duels between members and witnesses.

One was between Keynes and Sir Richard Hopkins, a high Treasury official. Keynes was trying to get Hopkins to defend or renounce the 'Treasury View'. This referred to a White Paper, *Memoranda on Certain Proposals Relating to Unemployment*, which the Conservative government had issued before the general election of 1929 and which criticised Lloyd George's election

---

[1] There is no report of Keynes' examination on these days in the *Minutes of Evidence*. For this, and for an account of the Macmillan Committee generally, see R. F. Harrod, *Life of John Maynard Keynes* (London, 1951), 413–26.

promises contained in *We can conquer unemployment*. Public works schemes to alleviate unemployment would, in the Treasury's view, diminish investment and employment 'in other directions'. Keynes, with some help from Bevin, tried to get Hopkins to admit that schemes of capital development would reduce unemployment, and that 'good' and 'bad' schemes (the latter promising little return on the sums spent) might be equally effective in creating work. Hopkins seemed to stick at four per cent as the rate of return which would justify a scheme. Keynes, besides touching on his idea of 'idle' money, was arguing that the interest rate which was determined by the foreign investment market—the current rate of interest, in fact—was not the right rate (i.e. was too high) to encourage home investment. The trouble with the method of eliciting facts and ideas by cross-examination, which is the method of any committee taking evidence, is that it is tedious and roundabout, and close reading of double-column folio pages is necessary to grasp the points being debated. Hopkins was the sole witness at two days' hearings, and the report occupies twenty-five of these pages (covering several other matters beside those just mentioned).

One passage may give the flavour of the exchange; though it must be added that Keynes was not always so successful in making a witness look silly.

[Keynes] Whatever you do, you increase the existing employment in some particular direction, do you not?
[Hopkins] Yes. And the type of remedy which I would like to find, if only I could, is a remedy which would increase the volume of work which was available for the depressed industries, or alternatively reduce the total installations of those industries to the existing volume of work, and scrap the redundant.
[Keynes] If you increased unemployment still further would you not expect prices to fall still more? Whenever you increase unemployment you reduce the demand for goods, and therefore lessen their price?
[Hopkins] Yes, that would be so.
[Keynes] Why are you so pleased with the reduction of prices which the present crisis has brought about so far?
[Hopkins] Of course you only say that because you know quite well

that I am not pleased. I am, on the contrary, no more pleased than you are.

[Keynes] You take objection to the cure of unemployment on the ground that it might have some effect on the raising of prices. That is what I understand?

[Hopkins] I am sorry, but my diagnosis is different. I should have thought what we want is some tendency which will create a rise of prices throughout the world to begin with, excepting here, so that we may follow in its wake.

Mr. Bevin: How can you do that?

[Hopkins] Not by a scheme of this kind.

[Bevin] How?

[Hopkins] I have suggested that a certain contribution has been made by the recent Government debt operations.

Mr. Keynes: You want all other countries to adopt plans which you wish to reject for your own?

[Hopkins] Yes, that might serve.[1]

The second passage of arms was between Keynes and Bevin (once again) and Montagu Norman, the Governor of the Bank of England, and again it brought out the conflict between the Bank's—and the City's—interest rates designed to preserve both the Bank's gold stocks and the City's functions as international banker and trader, and credit policies which might help to create employment. The return to the gold standard in 1925 at the pre-war parity of pound to dollar was one target, Bevin claiming that it had the effect of 'jamming' industry.

3343. *Mr. Bevin:* I would like at this particular point to ask Mr. Norman whether or not he does not think that the action of 1925 just made that jam in industry complete, when we as industrialists were given a task of adjusting to the point of 10 per cent. without notice and without any chance of even considering the question?[2] — I

---

[1] *Minutes of Evidence* taken before the Committee on Finance and Industry, Vol. II (1931), 22, questions 5634-40. I have supplied the names of the inter-locutors, which in the text itself are not always easy to follow.

[2] In this extract the text is reproduced as printed. Once a member of the Commission had started to ask questions, each numbered question is his until a change is shown. The answers, all in this case by Montagu Norman, begin with a dash — though sometimes dashes are also used in the normal grammatical way.

think the change of 1925—and I have no doubt we are both referring to the same change—

3344. Yes. —was inevitable, made at the right time, but, as the Chairman has said, certain misfortunes of one kind and another have subsequently intervened and have made any effect which that change of 1925 might have had far more difficult and serious, but I do not attribute the ills of industry in the main to that change, and had that change been made and not been succeeded by other things which have happened I do not think—

3345. But in view of the fact that it did involve facing the work-people of this country with a proportionate reduction of wages, did it not make the misfortunes that you describe absolutely inevitable? —No, I do not think so.

3346. That is what happened? —I do not think as a necessary consequence.

3347. How could it have been done? You are Governor of the Bank of England. I am a Trade Union Official. That is the point we had to face across the table. I am taking from 1921 up to the point of 1924: I am meeting the industrialists who do not know anything that is in the mind of the Bank of England on the financial policy of this country. . . . [Bevin recounted the negotiations for a new level of wages in the first period of deflation after 1921.] Suddenly the whole thing is upset by the steps taken in 1925 which throws every bit of work that the two parties in industry had done out of gear. We are faced with rising unemployment, bitter disputes, and a new level of wages to be fixed, without notice, without consideration, without guide, without any indication as to what its object is. I ask you, Mr. Norman, if industry is placed in a position like that, whether or not you do not think the misfortune of the jam is absolutely inevitable? —No, I do not, Sir.[1]

There are many other examples of reports on long-range subjects. The Royal Commission on Population (1944–9) was appointed at a time when the birth rate was rising after the low level of the early thirties, which had led demographers to predict a drop in population by the end of the century (by one estimate,

[1] Committee on Industry and Finance, *Minutes of Evidence*, Vol. I, 214, questions 3343–7.

to under 4½ million people in England and Wales by the year
2035). The Report, another textbook which reflected the
assumptions and methods of the experts of that time, was reassuring to those who feared too small or too large a populace in
the future, estimating a population of 45½ millions in Great
Britain in 2047. Already, the population figures make this guess
look ludicrously low. The British population in 1967 was 53½
millions.

A classic among reports, yet perhaps the most barren of results,
was the Report of the Machinery of Government Committee
chaired by Lord Haldane; the Committee was one among many
set up by the Ministry of Reconstruction in the latter part of the
First World War. The Report analysed the Cabinet and the
government departments, and examined two principles for
redistributing the latter's functions, by the groups of people they
served (e.g. children) or by the services they performed, preferring
the latter. In the scheme proposed there were to be departments of
finance, national defence and external affairs, research and information, employment, health, justice, education, supplies, production. Alas, none of these came into being for many years, except
for the Ministry of Health. Yet the Report, published in 1918, was
reprinted in 1948—for use by political scientists.

Reports on education have a much higher rating for achievement. The Hadow Report (the Board of Education, Consultative
Committee, *Report on the Education of the Adolescent*, 1926) recommended the 'break at eleven' (i.e., selection at eleven-plus), the
reorganisation of primary education, and a tripartite system of
secondary education. The latter proposal, elaborated by another
committee under Sir Will Spens in 1938, was the basis for the
organisation of secondary education in R. A. Butler's Education
Act of 1944. More recently the Robbins Report helped by its
blessing and its tables and projections the large expansion in the
number of students in higher education. The Public Schools
Commission, by contrast, has so far laboured without raising
anything except the temper of discussion.

The Second World War yielded its crop of committees peering

into the future, though it was a much smaller crop than the Ministry of Reconstruction's a quarter-century before. The Report on *Social Insurance and Allied Services* (the Beveridge Report of 1942) crystallised ideas and convictions, partly war-born, about the 'welfare state' and so helped to bring it into being in 1945–8. The Scott and Uthwatt Reports on *Land Utilisation in Rural Areas* (1942) and on *Compensation and Betterment* (1941) contributed to later policies of town and country planning. After the war Sir Stafford Cripps, at the Board of Trade, introduced the idea of the 'working party'; the reports of the many working parties on the state and prospects of the various industries are important documents for the immediate post-war years.[1] And so to the present output, 'Maud' on local government (1969), 'Fulton' on the civil service (1968), and 'Donovan' on the trade unions (1968). The tradition of great commissions and reports, with their varying fates, continues.

3. DOCUMENTS ON FOREIGN POLICY

In the field of foreign policy most governments have made an exception to their normal rules about the publication of documents from the official records. In matters of peace or war, when questions of guilt, blame, negligence may be raised and the consequences of decisions may affect thousands of lives, governments have felt the need to justify themselves as soon as possible. The Foreign Office has issued White Papers publishing selected documents on current issues or crises as a matter of course; these, as we have seen, form a part of the Parliamentary Papers.[2] It has also published a long series of *British Documents on the Origins of the War, 1898–1914* (edited by G. P. Gooch and H. W. V. Temperley, London, 1927–38). Other governments published similar series. For the origins of the Second World War it followed the same

---

[1] The Reports, published in 1946–8, covered seventeen industries, including Boots and Shoes, Furniture, Hosiery, Cotton, Linoleum, Wool, Clothing.

[2] For example, White Paper on the text of correspondence between British and German governments, 22–31 August 1939, published on 1 September 1939.

course, appointing two historians, Professor E. L. Woodward and Rohan Butler, as the first editors of *Documents on British Foreign Policy, 1919–1939*. The editors decided to make three borings, so to speak, into the mass of documents, making three series, I beginning in 1919, II in 1929 and III for 1938–9. The first volume appeared in 1946. Series III was completed in nine volumes between 1949 and 1955. The other series are still in process of publication, and a new series, IA, beginning at 1925, has been added. There is no intention, so far, of following this work by a similar undertaking for more recent years. In this the British government is sometimes compared unfavourably with the American. The *Foreign Relations of the United States* has traditionally published documents within a few years of their official use, but the American Historical Association has complained that the series has now fallen twenty-three years in arrears.[1]

Documents on British Foreign Policy can obviously contain only a selection from the vast mass of the Foreign Office archives. The editors, as they made clear in the prefaces of the volumes, were given access to all papers in the archives, and complete freedom in the selection and arrangement of documents. Obviously, without selection publication would be impossible; as it is, the series is long (and still incomplete), and each volume is massive. One must trust to the judgment and faith of the professional historians who have acted as editors in the choice of the documents printed and the authenticity of the texts; if one will not trust them and accept their assurances that no document was denied them and none of importance omitted, one can trust no historian's work. From time to time there is a controversy about the value of 'official history' and the freedom of official historians. No-one has proved that official historians are any different from other historians save in seeing official papers otherwise closed.[2] The point has been made, however, that the editors of *D.B.F.P.* have not published the minutes written upon or about the documents. It has also been observed that the series tells nothing of the internal working of the

---

[1] *American Historical Review*, 74: 1472 (April 1969).
[2] See below, pp. 186–7.

Foreign Office. Decisions were taken on what seems to have been faulty intelligence, for example in the May crisis of 1938 when it seemed as if Hitler was staging manœuvres preparatory to an invasion of Czechoslovakia, and the British government issued a warning which infuriated him.[1] Similarly, in March 1939 rumours of imminent German attacks on Poland and Roumania led the British government to the new policy of giving guarantees to possible victims of German aggression. The News Department, it is suggested, was also blameworthy for giving officials, press and public false ideas.[2]

In spite of these criticisms, *Documents on British Foreign Policy* provides a mass of raw material—the information on which the Foreign Office or the government acted in so far as it came from the embassies, legations and consulates abroad, and the observations and instructions despatched to British diplomatic officials in return. Deliberations and recommendations of the Cabinet, the reasons why Lord Halifax or Neville Chamberlain, for example, decided and acted as they did: it is no business of the series to give information on these matters.[3] To do so would be to take it far outside the Foreign Office and into the realms of politics and public opinion in general. The *Documents* are only one source, though an invaluable one, for reconstructing the history of British foreign policy. And they cannot be understood unless they are read in the light of some knowledge of the course of events, whether derived from histories of foreign policy or from other sources.

In themselves, the volumes of *D.B.F.P.* are austere. There is no introduction or commentary, and only a minimum of footnotes, mostly giving cross-references but occasionally abstracting or

[1] But see W. V. Wallace, 'The Making of the May Crisis of 1938', *Slavonic and East European Review*, XLI, 368–90 (June 1963) and the subsequent controversy between Wallace and D. C. Watt, ibid., XLIV, 475–86 (July 1966).

[2] These points are put with much weight by T. Desmond Williams in 'The Historiography of World War II', *Historical Studies I: Papers read before the Second Irish Conference of Historians* (London, 1958), 37–40.

[3] See the editor's note to *D.B.F.P.*, 3rd series, Vol. I (London, 1949), iv.

quoting from other documents not included in the series. There is a full analytical table of contents listing each document printed. The documents are arranged chronologically, so that at a time of crisis telegrams coming in from half a dozen capitals, and others despatched thereto, jostle each other indiscriminately. The original numbers of the telegrams and despatches, as well as the times of despatch and receipt, are given, and the reference to the location of the documents in the Foreign Office files.

This itself suggests something of what is to be found in the *Documents*. We might look at Volume II of the third series by way of illustration; this gives the documentary record of British policy in the crisis over Czechoslovakia in 1938 from the announcement of Lord Runciman's mission in July to the Munich agreement at the end of September. The first half of the story, from March onwards, appears in the previous volume.

The first half of the book has a leisurely air. There are quite lengthy despatches from Runciman, from Prague, from Berlin, where Sir Nevile Henderson was ambassador; a few from Paris. There are Lord Halifax's replies, and a few more personal letters exchanged between Halifax and Runciman. From the time of Hitler's speech at the Nazi party rally at Nuremberg on 12 September the pace quickened. Hitler railed against President Beneš and the Czechs, but without declaring war; a revolt by the Sudeten Germans went off prematurely and was suppressed; the danger of Hitler deciding to attack Czechoslovakia, with the risk of a general war developing, was great though uncertain. Chamberlain decided to put into effect a policy which he had been considering for the last two weeks of making personal contact with Hitler. Document 862, Viscount Halifax to Sir N. Henderson (Berlin), No. 368 Telegraphic: by telephone Foreign Office, 13 September 1938, encloses Chamberlain's brief personal message to be delivered to Hitler:

> In view of increasingly critical situation I propose to come over at once to see you with a view to trying to find peaceful solution. I propose to come by air and am ready to start tomorrow.

Please indicate earliest time at which you can see me and suggest place of meeting. Should be grateful for very early reply.

Neville Chamberlain.[1]

Chamberlain's meeting with Hitler at Berchtesgaden followed on 15 September. For this we have two versions: Chamberlain's notes of the conversation, and a much longer note (translated) by the German interpreter, Schmidt, obtained (with some difficulty: see Nos. 930, 931, 983, 985) from the German government. Three days later the French prime minister and foreign minister (Daladier and Bonnet) and other French officials came to London to hear Chamberlain's account of his meeting with Hitler, and to decide on a common policy. The report of these conversations at No. 10 Downing Street occupies twenty-seven pages. The argument was sharp, as the Frenchmen resisted the arguments of Chamberlain and his colleagues that Czechoslovakia must be put under the 'strongest pressure' to cede to Germany forthwith the disputed Sudeten areas lest war follow in which the French, though tied to Czechoslovakia by a treaty of alliance, would be unable to give any effective help. After the French had agreed we can see this pressure in Nos. 937 and 938, telegraphed from London to Newton, the British minister at Prague, at 2.45 a.m. and 11.30 a.m. on 19 September. The second read:

I wish to emphasize again the urgent need for a reply from President Beneš tonight or tomorrow. The Prime Minister's visit to Herr Hitler cannot be postponed beyond Wednesday, and he would be in a most difficult position, and indeed it might be disastrous, if he should have to go without any answer from Prague.

When the Czech government rejected the proposal an ultimatum was sent (No. 991, 21 September, 1.20 p.m.); by asking the government 'to consider urgently and seriously before producing a situation for which we could take no responsibility' it was warning the Czechs that they could expect no help from outside if they

[1] This letter was printed by Sir Keith Feiling in his *Life of Neville Chamberlain*, published in 1946 (three years before *D.B.F.P.*), 363.

rejected the advice. 'Please act immediately on receipt at whatever hour', Newton was told. The Czech government capitulated ('The Government's reply is affirmative . . .': No. 993 from Newton, received by the Foreign Office at 7.30 a.m. that morning, 21 September), but further pressure was needed (Nos. 998, 1000) before the final surrender at 5 p.m. (Nos. 1002, 1004).

This was not the end of the story. When Chamberlain met Hitler the second time, at Godesberg on 22 September, he found Hitler unsatisfied: the procedure proposed was too slow, German troops must march into the Sudeten areas immediately. The record of two meetings, on 22 September and the night of 23–24 September, is given in Nos. 1033 and 1073; these are lengthy and lively notes kept by a member of the Foreign Office, Ivone Kirkpatrick. At times the exchange in the dialogue between Hitler and Chamberlain was rapid, the remarks sharp:

> Herr Hitler maintained that if Czechoslovakia was sincerely determined to abide by her acceptance of the principle of self-determination, she would not mobilise.
> The Prime Minister asked who mobilised first?
> Herr Hitler said: The Czechs.
> The Prime Minister retorted that on the contrary Germany had mobilised first; she had called up reservists and moved troops to the frontier (pp. 501–2).

When Hitler produced his demands in a memorandum Chamberlain called it an ultimatum.

> Herr Hitler said it bore the word 'Memorandum' on the top. The Prime Minister retorted that he was more impressed by the contents than by the title (p. 504).

There was more pressure on the Czechs, which was rejected. There was another long round of Anglo-French conversations at No. 10 Downing Street on 25 to 26 September. There were warnings of ruin from the excitable Nevile Henderson. War seemed inevitable. Chamberlain sent his confidant, Sir Horace Wilson, on a last mission to Berlin, but his first meeting with

Hitler on 26 September went badly: 'very violent hour', began his telegraphic report (No. 1115). At a second meeting, on the 27th, however, he was able to get over to Hitler the warning from Chamberlain:

> I said that the future depended on the course of events in the next few days and next few weeks, which would decide how far the conflagration spread and then, in what I hope was the tone you would wish, delivered the message, very slowly (Wilson's report, No. 1128).

For the message we have to go to Kirkpatrick's notes of the conversation (No. 1129):

> The situation was as follows: if Czechoslovakia accepted [the Godesberg Memorandum], well and good. If she refused and Germany attacked Czechoslovakia, France, she had informed us, would feel that she must fulfil her treaty obligations. (Herr Hitler interjected once more, 'Which means that France must attack Germany.')
>
> Sir Horace Wilson continued by pointing out that he was using a particular form of words with care since it was the form employed by the French . . . if in fulfilment of these obligations France decided that her forces must be actively engaged (Herr Hitler interjected, 'To attack'), then, for reasons and grounds which would be clear to Herr Hitler and to all students of the international situation, Great Britain must be obliged to support her.

Hitler seemed adamant, but the interview ended quietly, and the long justificatory letter which he sent to Chamberlain that day (No. 1144) left a gleam of hope at the end. Seizing on this, Chamberlain sent a final note to Hitler at 11.30 a.m. on 28 September, invoking the help of Mussolini at the same time. The Munich conference of 29 to 30 September followed (reported in Sir H. Wilson's notes, No. 1227; text of agreement in No. 1225). Notes by Schmidt, the interpreter, of Chamberlain's conversation with Hitler in Hitler's flat in Munich late that night (30 September) and of the statement of goodwill which they both signed (and of which no official copy now exists in the Foreign Office archives) close the account (No. 1228). In all the documents in this volume occupy 692 pages.

Of course there is much else which the *Documents on British Foreign Policy* can yield. In the controversy between traditionalists and revisionists over the origins of the Second World War they can play an important part. The controversy turns on the nature of Hitler's aims and the degree to which he definitely planned (if he did) to make war on France and Britain, or on Russia; it turns partly on the extent of German rearmament as an indication of Hitler's plans. Hitler's 'war-guilt' has been argued from the 'Hossbach Memorandum' of a meeting between Hitler and members of the high command on 5 November 1937, in which he spoke of the necessity of solving Germany's 'need for space' and talked of war with Britain and France, 'two hate-inspired antagonists', in certain contingencies no later than 1943–5. He envisaged attacks on Austria and Czechoslovakia: 'the descent upon the Czechs would have to be carried out with "lightning speed".'[1] The authenticity of the document has been questioned,[2] and it was dismissed by A. J. P. Taylor as 'day-dreaming'.[3] But there are other documents pointing to Hitler's warlike intentions in *Documents on German Foreign Policy*, a series of captured German documents edited by American and English scholars; for instance, a memorandum by Hitler in August 1936 set forth a four-year plan to prepare for a major war.[4] A memorandum of 30 November 1938 spoke in similar terms.[5] And four months after Munich, in January 1939, the British government was informing the American, French and Belgian governments of intelligence that Hitler was considering an attack on Britain and France before beginning operations in eastern Europe; a surprise attack on

[1] *Documents on German Foreign Policy, 1918–1945*, series D, Vol. I (London, 1949), 29–39.
[2] H. W. Koch, 'Hitler and the origins of the Second World War', *Historical Journal*, XI, 125–43 (1968).
[3] A. J. P. Taylor, *Origins of the Second World War* (London, 1961), 131–4.
[4] W. N. Medlicott, *British Foreign Policy since Versailles, 1919–1963* (London, 1968), 173.
[5] *Documents on German Foreign Policy*, series D, Vol. IV, 529.

Holland and an air attack against Britain were contemplated, and the danger period would be at the end of February.[1] But how good was this intelligence? Desmond Williams' criticism, already quoted (p. 44) is apposite.

Diplomatic historians who study these questions naturally use far more sources than those to be found in *Documents on British Foreign Policy*. The documentary series published by other governments, foreign archives, contemporary newspapers and books on what were then current affairs, and the memoirs of politicians and diplomatic officials contribute to unravelling the chain of events.[2]

4. THE CENSUS AND THE REGISTRAR-GENERAL'S REPORTS

The Census of England and Wales, and of Scotland, taken every tenth year since 1801 (except for 1941), is likely to become even more important to the recent and contemporary historian than it has been to his predecessors. For in an age of ever-accelerating change, a regular ten-year stocktaking becomes even more vital for comparative purposes. The large volumes take several years to appear; and to bridge the ten-year gap a ten per cent *Sample Census* was conducted in 1966.

There are broadly three kinds of information which the Census can provide. The first is clearly the state of the population in the country as a whole (remembering that Scotland is treated separately from England and Wales): its size, distribution by sex and age, marital status, size of families. There are also migration tables and particulars of numbers of foreign and commonwealth residents. Secondly, the occupations of the people: from which, by comparing the figures in earlier censuses, one can see which

[1] *Documents on British Foreign Policy*, series III, Vol. IV, Nos. 5, 20, 40.
[2] For what can be got from memoirs see several of the essays in D. C. Watt, *Personalities and Politics: Studies in the Formulation of British Foreign Policy in the Twentieth Century* (London, 1965). See also W. V. Wallace's articles cited above, p. 44, footnote 1, and his 'Foreign Policy of President Beneš in the Approach to Munich', *Slavonic and East European Review*, XXXIX, 108–36 (December 1960).

occupations are rising in the numbers they absorb and which are declining. Third, the housing of the people, size of houses, number of persons per house or room, overcrowding. Most of the same information also is repeated in the county volumes. Here the figures are broken down for the county boroughs, municipal boroughs, urban and rural district councils, wards and villages. It is thus possible to see just where the population is declining, in which villages or local council areas, in which parts of the big cities; equally evident are the cities and counties which are growing, suburbs which are expanding, the occupations which are rising or declining locally. Studies of almost microscopic detail are possible. Tables showing place of birth give some indications of mobility. The number of Welsh-speaking people in Wales is given in a separate report.[1]

For the health of the nation one must turn to the work of the Registrar-General[2] who keeps the records of births, deaths and marriages. Here will be found the birth and death rate per 1,000 persons for the country as a whole, and for London, the county boroughs, urban and rural districts. The breakdown is carried even further, to individual districts, towns and rural areas, so that the differing chances of survival according to place of residence can be discovered. For example, if the over-all death rate for England and Wales in 1937 is given the index number of 100, the index number for Finsbury was 128, Croydon 90, Harrow 73; Manchester's was 128, Rhondda 134, but Exeter's was 90, Cambridge's 73. Comparisons with earlier years will show the degree to which life expectancy has increased.

The causes of death tell something of the strains of modern life and the advances of medicine. Tuberculosis was a killer until very recently. In 1922–5 the death rate from tuberculosis was 393 per one million population; by 1936–9 it was down to 216, by 1967

[1] For guidance see D. C. Marsh, *Changing Social Structure of England and Wales 1871–1961*, rev. ed. (London, 1965) and B. Benjamin, *The Population Census* (London, 1970).

[2] *Registrar-General's Statistical Review of England and Wales* (annual) and *Annual Report of the Registrar-General for Scotland*.

to 14. Again, the rate varied enormously from place to place, and was noticeably higher in 1937 in the areas of heavy unemployment. Other indices of public health are the figures of infant mortality (number of infants under one year dying per 1,000 live births) and of maternal mortality. Again, there are regional and local variations; for instance, infant mortality in Scotland was 80·3 in 1937 as compared with 58 in England and Wales.

Military service provided another standard for measuring the nation's health: the results of the medical examination of men called up for military service. Of the men examined in 1939–46, seventy per cent were placed in Grade 1, nine per cent in Grade 4 (unfit for any form of service). The figures for those under twenty-one, and aged twenty-one to twenty-five, which might be expected to show the results of under-nourishment in the depression years, were respectively eighty-one per cent and seventy-one per cent placed in Grade 1, five per cent and seven per cent in Grade 4. The record in the First World War had been quite different: of men examined in 1917–18 only thirty-six per cent were placed in Grade 1, 22·5 per cent in Grade 2, 31·5 per cent in Grade 3 and ten per cent in Grade 4 (1939–45 figures for Grades 2 and 3 were fourteen per cent and seven per cent.)[1]

5. ANNUAL AND SPECIAL REPORTS: LOCAL AND UNOFFICIAL

It is not only Her Majesty's Stationery Office which publishes documents of an official sort. Local authorities publish reports also, though the average member of the public seldom sees them. Reports of local medical officers of health provided the basis for one of the most interesting reports on the incidence of poverty in the inter-war years, G. C. M. M'Gonigle and J. Kirby, *Poverty and Public Health* (London, 1936). This gave a disheartening report of the effect of re-housing slum families on new housing estates in Stockton-on-Tees. Because of higher rents and fares and higher prices in the local shops, the re-housed families lived less well and

[1] Ministry of Labour and National Service, *Report for the Years 1939–1946* (Cmd. 7225: 1947).

showed higher death rates than their brethren who remained in the close-packed and outwardly insalubrious older districts.

Almost any organisation feels obliged to produce an annual report, though many of these are bare and formal, and others may leave unsaid the really important springs of action or clashes of personality behind the screen. Societies, companies, schools, universities, political parties all generate reports. Company reports to shareholders are seldom enlightening, and business histories which might tell much more seldom have much to say about recent times. Charles Wilson's *Unilever, 1945–1965* (London, 1968), following his *History of Unilever* (two vols., London, 1954) is an honourable exception. Of parties one thinks of political programmes and election manifestoes. The Labour Party has been the most enterprising in the production of statements of policy: for example, *Labour and the New Social Order* in 1918, *Labour and the Nation* in 1928, *For Socialism and Peace* in 1934. Equally important are the bulky annual reports of the Labour Party (including the Party Conference) and the Trades Union Congress. The Liberal Party's 'Yellow Book' (so called from its cover), *Britain's Industrial Future* (1928), was an ambitious and thorough study of Britain's industries and trade and finance conducted under a committee assembled by Lloyd George which included many of the leading economists of the day. It deserves to stand beside the reports of the government's Balfour Committee on Industry and Trade. The Fabian Society's pamphlets, continuing an honourable tradition of three-quarters of a century, are repositories of current facts and opinions which soon become history. The Welsh Nationalist Party, *Plaid Cymru*, has produced studies of the economic prospects of a Wales separated from England.

6. PARLIAMENTARY DEBATES

On the face of it, the *Parliamentary Debates*, often called 'Hansard' from the name of their former publisher, ought to be of great value to the historian of the twentieth century. Yet a bowing acquaintance is all that most recent historians are likely to have with the Commons' debates, let alone the Lords', and a moment's reflection will show why. Any debate—on the second reading of a bill, on the King's or Queen's speech at the opening of Parliament, on an adjournment—is a very lengthy thing to read, anything up to 100 or more double-column pages. In the case of a government bill, or a motion of censure, the debate has much of the air of a sham battle. A minister introduces the bill, giving the history and the reasons behind it, or at least some explanation of it. An opposition spokesman deploys the objections and criticisms. A number of members then speak, elder statesmen, back-benchers, a new member making his maiden speech. The Speaker tries to see that all parties and shades of opinion get a hearing; the Scottish or Welsh point of view may be elicited. In the end another opposition speaker and another government minister sum up, and the vote is taken. The result, though not the actual figures, is known in advance. The government, having a majority (otherwise it would not be the government) wins. Defeat can come only from a rebellion within the party, and dissidents, though they may abstain, do not bring down their party's government.

The *Debates* are, in fact, low-grade ore for the historian: the gold they yield is seldom worth the mass of rock to be worked through to get it. Better to read the main arguments, and the votes, in a newspaper. The inner history of the bill will not be in Hansard: the lobbying and building up of public opinion,[1] the government's soundings of interested parties, the briefs prepared by civil servants for their ministers, the decisions in Cabinet. Speeches in Parliament are merely the window-dressing. True, criticisms in the course of debate may lead to amendments to the bill; but to trace the history of these one needs to go, not to the *Debates*, but to the Minutes of Proceedings of the Standing Committees, which are published separately for each bill.

Of course there are exceptions, but they chiefly belong to times when a coalition government, or one without a proper majority, is in office. Thus the bill creating the Ministry of Transport, at

[1] S. E. Finer, *Anonymous Empire* (London, 1958, 2nd ed. 1966); J. D. Stewart, *British Pressure Groups* (Oxford, 1958).

first rather grandly called the Ministry of Ways and Communications Bill and introduced in 1919 by the government of Lloyd George, ran into much opposition. Some of it came from dissident Tory back-benchers such as Sir William Joynson-Hicks, an early protagonist of roads and road haulage as against the railways; the idea of roads being under the control of the same minister as railways, and presumably (he believed) subordinated to the railways, was anathema to him. Two speakers referred to a campaign of identical telegrams engineered by the road interests: 'we were wired to send telegrams', one constituent had told his member. Other speakers kept asking whether the bill was a step towards the nationalisation of railways, and the government yielded to the probing by modifying the clause giving the minister power to acquire railways and docks for a period up to two years.[1]

A rather different case is that of a private member's bill. Whether it becomes law or not, whether it originated in the Lords or Commons, such a bill, on a rather specialised subject, may get only brief treatment in the press. The student of, say, the reform of the laws relating to homosexuality or abortion will want to go to the relevant debates in 1967.

Then there is the rare debate which has some drama or passion about it, when the outcome is uncertain until the end and the vote causes a government's downfall. There have not been many of these since 1914; the main political crises involving a sudden change of government have been acted out away from Parliament (the Asquith coalition in 1915, Lloyd George's seizure of power in 1916, the fall of the Lloyd George coalition in 1922, the fall of the Labour government in 1931, the resignation of Harold Macmillan in 1963). There were two, however, in 1924. The first was in January, after the general election which had defeated the Conservatives under Stanley Baldwin but provided neither the Liberals nor Labour with a majority. Labour outnumbered the Liberals and moved an amendment to the Baldwin government's King's speech; the Liberals, led by Asquith, in one of his last

[1] *Parliamentary Debates:* 5th series, Vol. 113, *House of Commons* (cited as 113 H.C. Deb. 5 s.), cols 1761–1867, 1947–2060 (second reading).

major speeches in the House of Commons, supported the amendment and the government was defeated. The first Labour government followed. It fell in October when the Liberals and Conservatives joined in voting for a select committee to go into the government's handling of the 'Campbell case'—the withdrawal of proceedings against a Communist editor for a seditious article. Ramsay MacDonald's speech, a rather lame explanation of the facts, is important, but that of Sir Patrick Hastings, the Attorney-General, who had immediate responsibility in the case, carried the honours of the day.

A debate of far greater moment was that of 7–8 May 1940, following the disastrous Norwegian campaign, when Neville Chamberlain's majority was so reduced by Conservative abstentions and votes against the government that he resigned on 10 May, making way for Winston Churchill. There were several notable speeches, by Clement Attlee and Herbert Morrison for Labour, by Churchill and Chamberlain, by Admiral Sir Roger Keyes (speaking in full uniform), by Leopold Amery, the independent Conservative who borrowed Oliver Cromwell's words to the Long Parliament for his peroration: 'You have sat too long here for any good you have been doing. Depart, I say, and let us have done with you. In the name of God, go.' Finally there was Lloyd George, making what proved to be his last major speech in the House:

[The Prime Minister] has appealed for sacrifice. The nation is prepared for every sacrifice so long as it has leadership. . . . I say solemnly that the Prime Minister should give an example of sacrifice, for there is nothing which can contribute more to victory in this war than that he should sacrifice the seals of office.[1]

Among other critical debates there were those during the Suez crisis, in which the actual words used by Anthony Eden and the foreign secretary, Selwyn Lloyd, are crucial. There was the 'Maurice debate' on 9 May 1918, in which Lloyd George defended himself against the charge made by General Sir Frederick Maurice

[1] 360 *H.C. Deb.* 5 s., 1283 (8 May 1940).

that he had dangerously weakened Sir Douglas Haig's forces before the start of the German offensive in March. This was a battle of numbers; but it was only years later that it emerged that Lloyd George was unknowingly using incorrect figures supplied by the War Office, when Lord Beaverbrook quoted from the diary of Frances Stevenson (Lloyd George's secretary). A corrected set of figures had been found by another secretary at the bottom of a despatch box after Lloyd George's speech; he burnt it.[1] Many of the Asquith Liberals who voted against the government in the debate were subsequently proscribed by not getting Lloyd George's 'coupon' of endorsement at the 1918 general election.

Yet another debate of great consequence was that which took place some weeks after the Easter Rising in Dublin of 24 April 1916. Because of the confusion and blackout of news it took a long time before the British public learned something of the character of the rising and of the vengeance which General Maxwell, the commanding officer, was exacting after courts martial of the leaders. It was the Irish Nationalist members (the Home Rulers), soon to be repudiated by their fellow-countrymen, who brought out the facts of the murder, by a mad British officer, of an innocent citizen of Dublin, the well-known writer, Francis Sheehy-Skeffington. On 11 May John Dillon, in perhaps his greatest speech in Parliament, told the full story and told also of the effect of the executions in turning the Irish public from opposition to the rebels to support for them. This was the first rebellion 'in which the Irish majority was on your side. It is the fruit of our life's work [the work of the Home Rulers to achieve a constitutional settlement through Parliament]. We have risked our lives a hundred times to bring about this result. We are held up to odium as traitors by those men who made this rebellion, and our lives have been in danger a hundred times during the last thirty years because we have endeavoured to reconcile the two things, and now you are washing out our whole life work in a sea of blood.'[2]

Another use of the *Debates* is for the texts of speeches by the

[1] Lord Beaverbrook, *Men and Power* (London, 1956), 262–3.
[2] 82 *H.C. Deb.* 5 s., 940.

leading members, or for the tone of their speeches. Here, of course, we have to remember the 'House of Commons style', which is informal, almost conversational. Perhaps Churchill's best speeches were made in Parliament; for instance, his speech after the sacrifice of Czechoslovakia at Munich: 'we have sustained a total and unmitigated defeat.' MacDonald in his day was a formidable parliamentarian, better in opposition than in office. Baldwin was master of the apparently impromptu set speech: his 'peace in our time' speech of 6 March 1925 opposing a Conservative private member's bill to change the trade unions' political levy in a way which would hurt the Labour Party. There was his speech recounting the circumstances which led to King Edward VIII's abdication (10 December 1936). Less happy was his 'appalling frankness' speech of 12 November 1936 in which he seemed to be answering charges of delay in rearmament by the plea that he would have lost the election by advocating a faster pace; this was the basis of Churchill's charge in his memoirs,[1] that he had put party before country.

Everyone will have his favourite speaker, and can follow him through the volumes of the *Debates*. He may be one of the leaders of the day. He may be a picturesque individualist like James Maxton of the I.L.P. (his speech implying that members who voted for reductions in grants to child-care centres were murderers, for which he and three other Clydesiders were suspended, was on 28 June, 1923). Or he may be an obscure back-bencher whose career someone is studying. Equally, one may want to see, from their speeches, the interests of a group of members—businessmen, or members representing the universities (before the abolition of the university seats), or Scottish members, trade union members, independents. The division lists, though they tell little in times of effective party discipline, may on occasion reveal cross-voting, defections or abstentions, and are certainly revealing on a 'free vote'. But the journalists will often have done the sums of this sort, and published them, at the time.

[1] W. S. Churchill, *The Second World War*, I, *The Gathering Storm* (London, 1948), index s.v. Baldwin.

There is another way in which the *Debates* can be an important source: in reporting parliamentary questions with the ministerial answers, 'supplementaries' and replies, and also the written answers to questions. How to winkle out information, how to trip up a minister—this has been for many members a fine art. Almost any matter, weighty or trivial, may call it forth: the Suez campaign, Tory baiting of MacDonald at the time of the Campbell case when he seemed, by answers on successive days, to be concealing the facts and when he was irritated by questions about the motor-car given him, with an endowment in shares, by Sir Alexander Grant of McVitie and Price, the biscuit manufacturers (hence the taunt, 'biscuits', which he resented). Again MacDonald was involved, along with Philip Snowden, in a series of answers in September 1931 about the 'conditions of borrowing' to save the pound, just before the fall of the Labour government in August, which the New York bankers had allegedly imposed. Had the bankers insisted on a reduction of payments to the unemployed? MacDonald on 21 September mentioned 'special conditions of borrowing' of this sort; Snowden denied that there were any such conditions.

Whatever you want in the *Debates* should at least be easy, if tedious, to find. The volumes are admirably indexed together with a separate index volume at the end of each session. Not only the names of members speaking, but the whole range of subjects debated or touched on in questions, are given.

The texts of statutes which are the fruits of parliamentary debates are in the series *Public General Acts* published annually by government. The practice of citing acts by the regnal year in which they were enacted was abandoned in 1963 and the calendar year substituted. Thus the Public Records Act of 1967 is cited as 1967, chapter 44; under the former method of citation it is 15 and 16, Eliz. II, ch. 44. Private and local acts (now called local and personal) are published in a separate series.

CHAPTER 3

Cabinet and Other Papers

I. CABINET RECORDS

Until 1966 British historians worked under the handicap of the 'fifty-year rule'. All government records, whether transferred to the Public Record Office or kept in the originating department, were closed to researchers until fifty years had elapsed 'from the date of the last paper in the piece'—a piece being a single sheet, file, volume, box or bundle.[1] The historian embarking on any research into British history since 1914 could not see any of the government's records until 1 January 1965, and then only for 1914. A year later he could begin work on those of 1915, and so on.

Even this restriction was an improvement on previous practice. Until the Public Records Act of 1958 there was no automatic opening of the fifty-year old records year by year, though a fifty-year rule was supposedly in force: openings took place only at irregular intervals. The 1958 Act also provided a standard procedure for the review, weeding and transfer of papers from departments to the Public Record Office, with a review of the working of the new procedure after five years.[2]

The change to the present thirty-year rule came only with the advent of the Labour government, and then only after some delay. A campaign was begun by a group of historians from Oxford, Cambridge and London in 1963. They were irritated by the fact that Anthony Eden (Lord Avon) had clearly had access to recent government records in the compilation of his memoirs, and that protests against such favouritism while the general ban stood had been rejected with contempt by Harold Macmillan, as Prime

[1] Public Record Office, *Classes of Departmental Papers for 1906–1939* (London, 1966), q.v.

[2] D. C. Watt, 'Contemporary History: Problems and Perspectives', *Journal of the Society of Archivists*, III, 516 (October, 1969).

Minister. A delegation was received by the Cabinet Office. A more liberal spirit began to appear in some government departments, and the British Museum abandoned its own fifty-year rule which it had been applying to private papers given to it.[1]

The first breach of the fifty-year rule was announced by the Prime Minister, Harold Wilson, in Parliament on 10 February 1966: in order that the First World War and the post-war period could be studied as a whole, the records would be opened for the years 1916–22 in one fell swoop. This was a holding operation while a new policy was being framed. The government decided that its records should be opened after thirty years, and this was subsequently enacted by the Public Records Act of 1967.[2] To put it into effect the records for 1923–37 were opened on 1 January 1968. Since then the records for successive years have been opened year by year each January, those for 1938 on 1 January 1969, and so on. The main interest in these newly opened government archives centres on the records of the Cabinet, though in time the papers of the Foreign Office and the other departments will certainly be heavily used for scholarly monographs. In a sense there were no Cabinet records before December 1916, though the Cabinet itself, in some form or other, had over two centuries of history by then. Since it grew out of meetings of the 'confidential servants of the crown', sometimes over dinner, informality long hung about it. The only record of its discussions and decisions was the prime minister's letter to the sovereign, written, as Asquith continued to do to the end, in his own hand. There were of course many Cabinet papers, almost always printed, which were circulated among the members; of these, again, no official sets were kept, though the Foreign Office library had a large number on foreign affairs. This deficiency did not apply to the Committee of Imperial Defence; from its foundation in 1902 it kept all its records.

The lack of official Cabinet minutes and sets of papers did not prevent historians from discovering much of what went on in the Cabinet. The prime minister's letters to the sovereign might be

[1] *Ibid.*, 517–18. Mr Watt was a leading figure in the campaign.
[2] 1967, Chapter 44.

consulted in the Royal Archives at Windsor; private notes or reports in letters and diaries and private copies of Cabinet papers might be found among the family papers of former statesmen, either preserved among the family muniments or presented to a library. Research has now been greatly simplified by the enterprise of the Public Record Office in assembling from the Royal Archives photo-copies of the prime ministers' letters from 1886 to 1916; these now form the series Cab. 41.[1] Similarly, photo-copies of Cabinet papers, assembled from several sources, have been formed into another series, Cab. 37; for these the P.R.O. has published two guides, *List of Cabinet Papers, 1880–1914* (London, 1964) and *List of Cabinet Papers 1915 and 1916* (London, 1966). The guide for 1915 and 1916 also includes the papers of the War Council, the Dardanelles Committee and the War Committee which in succession filled the role which the Committee of Imperial Defence had held in peace-time. These are part of the series, Cab. 41, though the papers will also be found (as the guide shows) distributed through other Cabinet series.[2]

The modern Cabinet, with the Cabinet Office and secretaries, agenda, minutes, files, dates from the coming of Lloyd George to the prime ministership in December 1916. A small War Cabinet was created, together with a secretariat headed by Sir Maurice Hankey, who had been secretary of the Committee of Imperial Defence and its successors. Save that the War Cabinet was replaced by a normal and larger Cabinet in 1919 the arrangements inaugurated in 1916 have continued.[3]

For the work of the Cabinet there are four groups of papers to be consulted.[4] The first is Cab. 23, the Minutes (of the War Cabinet) or Conclusions (the term used for minutes when the Cabinet replaced the War Cabinet in 1919). This is obviously a

[1] The P.R.O.'s index of this has been published by the List and Index Society (Vol. 5).

[2] *List of Cabinet Papers 1915 and 1916*, vii and Appendix B.

[3] For the *working* of the Cabinet Secretariat from its inception see Thomas Jones, *Whitehall Diary*, I, *1916–1925*, ed. R. K. Middlemas (Oxford, 1969).

[4] What follows is based largely on the admirable, brief guide, *The Records of the Cabinet Office to 1922*, published by the Stationery Office as Public Record

long and continuing series. There are indexes in the Search Room
to the War Cabinet Minutes and the Cabinet Conclusions, as well
as an index to each volume. During the years 1916–19 the minutes
were kept in two series, ordinary and 'Secret'. These are both in
Cab. 23 but in different volumes, so that both series need to be
used together: the ordinary series is Cab. 23/1 to 23/12 (i.e.
Cabinet, class 23, volume 12), the secret series Cab. 23/14 to 23/17.
Cab. 23/18 and later volumes are the Cabinet Conclusions of
1919 onwards, but there was also a separate secret series in 1919
constituting Cab. 23/35. Also, Lloyd George, while prime
minister, used to hold some meetings which, while really Cabinets,
were called Conferences: they were less formal, and were very
fully reported, in contrast to the economy of the Cabinet Conclusions; these, for 1919–22, form Cab. 23/37 to 23/39.[1]

Second are the Cabinet papers or memoranda which formed the
basis of the Cabinet's discussions, and which must be consulted
along with the Conclusions. A very large number of these are in a
big general series, Cab. 24. They were referred to in War Cabinet
days as G and GT: each paper had a number in one or other of the
series, but both series co-existed chronologically and both should
be consulted for any given subject. There is a subject index for the
G and GT series in the Search Room. With the restoration of the
Cabinet the memoranda were numbered in a C.P. (Cabinet
Papers) series, for which there are also subject indexes. The
Cabinet Conclusions refer to the memoranda presented to any
particular meeting, which provides a clue to what to look for in
the C.P. series (Cab. 24).[2]

Office Handbooks No. 11 in 1966, at the time of the opening of the records to
1922. It contains a good, short history of the Cabinet and Secretariat. Much
which it says applies equally to the records after 1922. I am also greatly indebted
to Professor Paul B. Johnson for notes based on his extensive use of the Cabinet
records for 1917–21.

[1] The List and Index Society has published the Subject Index to Cab. 23, the
War Cabinet Minutes, December 1916–March 1918 (vol. 40) and April 1918–
October 1919 (vol. 52).
[2] The List and Index Society has published three volumes of the Subject Index
to Cab. 24 as its volumes 29, 41, 52, covering the C.P. series for 1919–22.

This is not the end of the trail, however. Many of the memoranda before the Cabinet come from Cabinet committees, both *ad hoc* and standing. The guide, *The Records of the Cabinet Office to 1922*, lists the many committees created in 1917–22, and the references by which each can be found. The more important were those on War Policy, Economic Offensive, Demobilisation, Industrial Unrest (which at the time of the railway strike of 1919 became the Strike Committee and later the Supply and Transport Committee), Finance, Unemployment, Ireland. Most of these committees' papers are in the large class, Cab. 27. Certain committees, however, have their own class: War Trade (Cab. 39), War Priorities (Cab. 40), Post-war Priority and Demobilisation (Cab. 33) and Home Affairs (Cab. 26).

The fourth group of Registered Files (Cab. 21) is small, since most of its contents are now in Cab. 24; what remains relates to the Cabinet machinery and secretariat, the Committee of Imperial Defence, and other bodies. There are also the papers of various conferences: the Supreme War Council, the Paris Peace Conference, the Washington Conference on Disarmament, the Imperial and Imperial War Conferences, and conferences on Ireland. These have their own class numbers, which are given in the guide.

Research in the Cabinet papers has been further simplified by the action of the Public Record Office in putting these papers in a separate Search Room, in which the various indexes will be found. Armed with the guide, a knowledge of the subject he wishes to investigate, and intelligence in the use of the indexes, the enquirer soon gets the hang of what sounds very complex in exposition, and can ask for the volumes he needs and find his way to the Cabinet meetings or papers he is concerned with. The main thing to remember is that material on one subject may be in several different classes, or in widely separated volumes in the same class. Thus for the history of housing in 1919–21 one must go (besides using the minutes or conclusions in Cab. 23 and the many papers in Cab. 24) to the Home Affairs Committee (Cab. 26/1), the Demobilisation Committee (27/41, 27/42, 27/49 and Cab. 33), and to the Conference volume 23/39 for the dismissal of the Minister, Christopher Addison. The papers of committees specifically on housing, shown in the guide, are in 27/56, 27/66, and 27/89 (also 27/132).[1]

In the future, research in the Cabinet papers may be made easier still by the preparation of a guide for their contents which is being sponsored by the Social Science Research Council and conducted from the University of Kent.

What difference will this new source of information, the Cabinet papers, make to the hitherto accepted narrative of events or ascription of causes? The answer in part is that we cannot know until research in the papers has shown its fruits in new books or articles on old subjects. That it will deepen our knowledge of what happened, and of the information on which ministers or Cabinet decided to act, is clear enough; but what the papers do not say, about motives or passions, the information they failed to supply to the government, will remain important, and light on these things will still have to be sought elsewhere. It is a truism that there are few secrets in government; one might almost say that the Official Secrets Act exists to conceal the fact that the cupboard is bare. It may be exciting to go through Cabinet files marked 'Secret. (This document is the property of His Britannic Majesty's Government)'; it may be disillusioning.

To take one instance. After the Easter rising in Dublin in 1916 Asquith's coalition government entrusted Lloyd George with the task of bringing the Home Rulers and Unionists together so that Home Rule (postponed in 1914) could be put into operation in some form at once. The plan came near to success, but was shot down by some Conservative members of the Cabinet. The course of events, and the documents which influenced decisions, can be traced in the Cabinet papers in Cab. 37, and it is useful to have the full text of a memorandum by Asquith of 19 May, of Lansdowne's and Long's memoranda of 21 and 23 June and General Maxwell's of 24 June. But the story had been pretty fully told by Lloyd

[1] For the example from housing, I am indebted to Professor Paul B. Johnson.

George himself in his *War Memoirs* (London, 1933–6) and in other accounts, such as Addison's *Four and a Half Years* (London, 1934), based on his diaries. Lloyd George is not the only minister who has retained documents after leaving office or who has been able to consult them. Politicians writing in these circumstances are expected to submit their manuscript to the Cabinet Office for vetting (as Lloyd George did), and the main convention followed is to exclude names and direct quotations—a convention which does not preclude quite a full account. The Cabinet papers for 1916 also give the reports of the Inspector-General of the Royal Irish Constabulary on the state of Ireland; but the Irish government has now published from its archives the much fuller *Intelligence Notes*[1] which were compiled and printed in the chief secretary's office in Dublin from the Inspector-General's monthly reports.

However, books are beginning to appear which show how much fuller history can be written from the Cabinet papers. One is Professor Paul B. Johnson's *Land Fit for Heroes: the Planning of British Reconstruction 1916–1919* (Chicago, 1968). Here is a detailed, exhaustive study of plans for reconstruction and their failure—or at least their limited success—based on the Cabinet papers, together with the papers of the Board of Trade, Ministers of Health and Munitions and the Ministry of Reconstruction, and the *Parliamentary Papers*. If the main outlines of the subject have not been changed, the emphasis has. Lloyd George, far from forwarding reconstruction, seems to have set it back when he changed the *modus operandi* from Asquith's Reconstruction Committee to a ministry. The detailed story of the failure of Addison's housing programme is set forth for the first time; in fact, the narrative of decontrol in 1919–21 has never been given so fully. And it is a complex story, involving the emotional campaign for nationalisation of the coalmines and other industries. The failure of the National Industrial Conference of 1919 is now fully documented. Some reputations rise in the scale: Addison, Auckland

[1] *Intelligence Notes 1913–16, preserved in the State Paper Office*, ed. Breandán Mac Giolla Choille (Dublin, Stationery Office, 1966).

Geddes, Sir Robert Horne as Minister of Labour. And the voices still sound (as they do not, alas, in the more austere style of Cabinet papers after 1922). Here is a report of a meeting between Lloyd George and a deputation of the Miners' Executive in October, 1919. Lloyd George asked whether some form of workers' control in the mining areas would not be acceptable: the alternative was not nationalisation but the restoration of private ownership. The miners rejected this as 'setting up trusts between the miners and the mineowners . . . against the general public'. William Brace said:

> The War has driven us 25 years at least in advance of where we were in thought in 1914. Our men have come to the conclusion that they are something infinitely more majestic than wage-earners. They have grasped a kind of soul-stirring idea that human life is very sacred, and in the future industrial economy of this Nation they must have their part.

Lloyd George replied:

> I think Labour is throwing away a great opportunity of having an effective voice . . . in the control of its own industry, and I do not see how it would stand ultimately in the way of nationalisation.[1]

Other examples of what may be garnered from the Cabinet papers are richly provided in Richard H. Ullman's *Britain and the Russian Civil War November 1918–February 1920* (Princeton, 1968), the second volume of Professor Ullman's study of Anglo-Soviet relations in 1917–21. The author explains in his preface that he had completed the first draft of his book in 1965, but the abrogation of the fifty-year rule in 1966 opened up completely new material, not only in the Cabinet papers but in the Curzon and Balfour papers which were liberated under the same change of rule. He courageously scrapped his draft, and after research in the new sources wrote a completely new book. He benefited from the fullness of the papers and reports of meetings in those brave

---

[1] Paul B. Johnson, *Land Fit for Heroes* (Chicago, 1968), 478–9.

pioneering days of the Cabinet Office. He is able to give the thoughts and arguments about British intervention in the Russian civil war from the memoranda of Sir Henry Wilson, Balfour and others in November 1918.[1] He can report fully on the deliberations of the Cabinet's Eastern Committee (in Cab. 27), noting under a meeting of 2 December 1918, that for its meetings 'the highly unusual practice was followed of making a shorthand record, and a verbatim transcript of each discussion was printed as an annex to the usual brief third-person minutes of the session. These verbatim transcripts are a uniquely valuable source for the historian: they offer not only the usual record of decisions taken, but insight into the argument and methods of thought employed by each participant.'[2] The rise and fall of Churchill's influence in support of intervention can be charted from his first appearance in the Imperial War Cabinet in December 1918. Lloyd George's realism and good sense are brought out.[3] And when the government was alarmed about public opinion over the continuance of fighting and conscription, and was apprehensive of industrial unrest on this score, it had the sensible reports of Sir Basil Thomson, Director of Intelligence at the Home Office, in the 'Fortnightly Reports of Revolutionary Organisations in the United Kingdom and Morale Abroad' (G.T. 6713: Cab. 24/74).[4]

The life of Stanley Baldwin published in 1969 is the first biography of a recent politician to make full, even exhausting, use of the Cabinet papers. From this source it is possible to show, for example, that Baldwin took a much larger part in forwarding rearmament in 1934–7 than has hitherto been realised. Unfortunately, the book provides no references for the Cabinet papers used; the reader is expected to be able to find the relevant documents from the dates of meetings supplied in the book.[5]

An example, showing how the Cabinet papers may confirm rather than transform the accepted story, comes from the General Strike of 1926. A critical question has been why the government

[1] R. H. Ullman, *Britain and the Russian Civil War* (Princeton, 1968), 10–18.
[2] *Ibid.*, 67, n. 21.   [3] *Ibid.*, 87, 90–3.   [4] *Ibid.*, 132.
[5] R. K. Middlemas and J. Barnes, *Baldwin* (London, 1969).

broke off the last-minute negotiations with a committee of the
T.U.C. on Sunday night, 2 May, which might have averted the
General Strike, and whether the break was planned in advance.
Since the excuse for the break was a telephone message that the
machine men at the *Daily Mail* office had refused to print next
day's leading article (it did in fact appear in some editions), and
Baldwin saw the T.U.C. committee, and handed them a letter
announcing the end of negotiations, less than an hour after they
had left him to consult among themselves, it was reasonable to
infer that a break had been prepared for beforehand; indeed
G. M. Young, in his life of Baldwin, had written that the Cabinet
had 'approved a note to be issued after that meeting [the meeting
of Baldwin and the T.U.C. representatives] if Ministers thought it
desirable'.[1] The Cabinet Conclusions confirm that this is what
happened. The Cabinet met at 6.45 that evening[2] and approved a
document breaking off negotiations (the text is given as an
appendix) 'for communication to the Committee of the Trades
Union Council, if after 9 p.m. interview this was deemed desirable'. During a second meeting of the Cabinet, at 9.30,[3] information of the *Daily Mail* incident was received

> and it was agreed that negotiations could not be continued without a
> repudiation by the Trades Union Council Committee of the actions
> referred to and unconditional withdrawal of the instructions for a
> general strike. The document approved at the previous meeting was
> accordingly re-drafted to meet the new situation and the Cabinet
> agreed—
> That the Prime Minister should communicate to the Trades Union
> Council Committee the document attached to the Appendix.

The appendix gives the re-drafted text. The Conclusions also
show that the code telegram 'Action' to put the government's

[1] G. M. Young, *Stanley Baldwin* (London, 1952), 114. See my *Britain between
the Wars* (London, 1955), 306–10, 314, for a narrative of these events. This
should now be supplemented by Lord Citrine's account in his memoirs, *Men
and Work* (London, 1964), 171–2.

[2] Cabinet 22 (26), i.e. the 22nd Cabinet meeting of 1926: the reference is
Cab. 23/52.

[3] Cabinet 23 (26) in Cab. 23/52.

strike plans into action was sent out to the civil commissioners and local authorities during the 6.45 p.m. Cabinet meeting by the Home Secretary, who 'left the Cabinet for a few minutes for this purpose'.

The Cabinet Conclusions also take us a little further back in following the Cabinet's line of reasoning. There was an earlier Cabinet that Sunday, at noon, at which ministers were expecting to hear from the T.U.C. committee what answer the miners had given to a 'formula' worked out on Saturday night between the T.U.C. and Baldwin and two of his colleagues. The T.U.C. failed to get in touch with the Prime Minister on Sunday morning (having discovered that the members of the miners' executive had dispersed to the various coalfields), which left the Cabinet to consider the growing likelihood of a general strike. A part of the Conclusions of that meeting, marked 'To H.M. only, not circulated in Minutes. M. A. P. H[ankey]', makes it clear that ministers were dissatisfied with the vagueness of the formula and the uncertain outcome of the negotiations, and felt that negotiations 'in conjunction with the menace of a general strike' would seem to the public to be a yielding to threats. They wanted a definite assurance that the miners would 'make some sacrifice', that is, accept lower wages, which was the crux of the dispute, and they argued that the complete withdrawal of the threat of a general strike was '*sine qua non* to any resumption of negotiations involving a subsidy' (to tide over the crisis in the mines). There was also a discussion with the Postmaster-General (who attended though not a member of the Cabinet) concerning the Supply and Transport Organisation. The Postmaster-General told the Cabinet that telegrams had been sent out to various unions calling for a 'cessation of work'. The Cabinet (somewhat disingenuously, one feels, since it was also making contingent arrangements for the General Strike) thought that 'the dispatch of these telegrams constituted a new factor which had an important bearing' on the discussion earlier in the meeting.[1] It is from the Conclusions of this noon meeting, in fact, that we can see how opinion

[1] Cabinet 21 (26): Cab. 23/52.

in the Cabinet had hardened before the 6.45 p.m. meeting.

The Cabinet memoranda (C.P. series, Cab. 24) also include several papers on the general strike and its preliminaries; there is, for instance, a long stenographic report of the futile discussions between Baldwin and the miners and mineowners on March 24 (Cab. 24/179/31). There are papers about a 'Civil Constabulary Reserve', proposed trade union legislation, and the Supply and Transport organisation, in various volumes in Cab. 27, and others from the Home Affairs Committee in Cab. 26. The researcher will also need to examine the Home Office papers and those of the War Office, Admiralty, and other departments.

Later examples of what the Cabinet papers reveal have been produced annually around 1 January, when journalists give a preview of the contents of the papers of the year about to be opened. From the papers for 1938, for example, we are given an account of Anthony Eden's resignation as foreign secretary in February; what is new are the names and views of members who spoke in Cabinet about whether to start negotiations with Mussolini or not, which was the point at issue.[1] The fact that the Cabinet was not unanimous, and that Duff Cooper, Oliver Stanley, Malcolm MacDonald and Walter Elliot were often critical of Chamberlain's policy, was already known.[2] Similarly, there is nothing new in revelations about Neville Chamberlain's actions which led up to Munich, and particularly the intense pressure put by the British and French governments to persuade the Czechs to surrender the Sudeten territories to Germany immediately: much of this was known at the time, or very soon after, and is fully documented from the Foreign Office papers in *Documents on British Foreign Policy*, series III, volume II, published in 1949.[3]

[1] M. Arnold-Foster, 'When Eden walked out', *Guardian*, 1 January 1969.

[2] Anthony Eden, *Facing the Dictators* (London, 1962), 590–5; Colin Coote, *A Companion of Honour: the story of Walter Elliot* (London, 1965), 165–71.

[3] 'How we helped Hitler', *Guardian*, 1 January 1969. For *D.B.F.P.* material, see above, pp. 43 ff.

2. OTHER GOVERNMENT DOCUMENTS

The introduction of the thirty-year rule has, of course, opened many other papers in the government's archives for the historian. These are the departmental papers: Treasury, Admiralty, Home Office, Foreign Office, Colonial Office and the rest. There is a short guide, *Classes of Departmental Papers for 1906–1939*.[1] This is almost as laconic as its title, but it is none the less a help because it gives the brief title of the subject of each class; for example, Ministry of Health, M.H. 68, is Poor Law Authorities 1904–1933, 425 'pieces'. Many of the classes are more fully described in the standard *Guide to the Contents of the Public Record Office* (1963), including now, in Vol. III, classes transferred between 1960 and 1966 which include many of the records for the 1920s and 30s. Obviously some classes have not been transferred at all, and possibly are of no historical importance; with the vast mass of paper which government departments generate, a programme of sorting and destruction is essential, and the chief danger is that it will be unintelligently done. The Public Record Office constantly gives advice to the departments on this matter.

This problem of 'weeding' is part of the wider problems of selection of papers for transfer to the P.R.O. and the availability for research of papers not transferred. Historians were encouraged by the fact that some of their number were invited to a conference of record officers (civil servants) from seventy-seven government departments in May 1968 which was concerned with the problem of selection of papers, or classes of papers, for preservation. Unfortunately, there are doubts whether civil servants of the necessary scholarly qualifications and seniority are entrusted with the vital tasks of review and selection.[2]

The question of availability of government papers (within or outside the closed period) has been taken up by a committee of the Social Science Research Council appointed in 1967. The

[1] P.R.O. Handbooks, No. 10 (London, 1966).
[2] D. C. Watt, *Journal of Society of Archivists*, III, 520–1.

Council is sponsoring the preparation of a guide to data for social scientists in the possession of the government, and specialised guides to particular subjects may also be forthcoming from this source.[1]

Another difficulty arises from the loss of documents. It is surprising that the Foreign Office does not have the original copy (*its* original copy, that is) of the Zinoviev Letter. Nor, much more serious, does it have the original of the Foreign Office draft of the protest sent to the Russian government about the Letter. Since this contained amendments in MacDonald's handwriting, and since he had a peculiar system of adding passages without crossing out passages he was discarding, a vital piece of evidence was lost when the Foreign Office destroyed the original, keeping only a typed copy.[2] The nub of MacDonald's complaint was that the Foreign Office published the protest before he had seen and authorised the final draft. Another missing original is that of the declaration of friendship signed by Hitler and Neville Chamberlain on the night of the Munich treaty.

It does not follow that papers transferred to the Public Office, and falling within the thirty-year rule, are necessarily open for research; any 'sensitive' subject is likely to be closed for fifty, seventy-five or even 100 years. Anglo-Irish relations in 1916–22 are, as one might expect, a case in point. Colonial Office classes 903 and 904 are on Ireland. Consulting the list for these classes in the search room one finds that a number of 'pieces' are closed, and of these no description is given, nor any indication of the size of each 'piece'; thus of the Dublin Castle Records (C.O. 904), 904/24–26 and 193–216 are closed for seventy-five years, 904/6, 36, 40–4 and 156 (Part II) are closed for 100 years. One can infer from the place of the closed 'pieces' in the sequence of open, listed papers that the subject matter of much, at least, of the closed papers is the raw material for 'Intelligence Notes'. In the War Office class 35, the class for Ireland, many 'pieces' are closed but listed.

[1] *Ibid.*, 522.
[2] T. Jones, *Whitehall Diary*, I (Oxford, 1969), 299. See below, ch. 8.

None the less, there is plenty of material (even on Ireland) which is now open. To find it, the brief advice in Handbook No. 10 cannot be bettered. Decide in which departments you may expect to find information, bearing in mind that a subject may have been transferred from one department to another several times; the Handbook gives shipping as an example, for the Board of Trade, Admiralty, Shipping, War Transport and Transport each had jurisdiction in turn. Then find the relevant classes in the department's papers, and look up the class list in the search room; this describes each 'piece' and so tells you what to ask for.[1]

3. PRIVATE PAPERS

For many English historians, particularly of the eighteenth and nineteenth centuries, working in the private papers of some long deceased statesman or minor politician has been a large and pleasant part of research. Much of the glamour of this is in the mind: the hero-historian discovers all-important manuscripts in an old trunk in an attic or stables, or works through bundles of faded letters in the stately library or dark muniment room of a great country house. Very hard and often unrewarding work is the reality.

The twentieth-century historian also has the opportunity of using the private papers of politicians. Present-day governments are much stricter in the interpretation of private. While in the past statesmen kept their official papers and files, and so left them ultimately among their muniments (as Presidents of the United States today leave their papers in especially endowed libraries), nowadays the government attempts to recover all official papers from former ministers. Indeed, the lengths to which the government will go in pursuit were shown by Raymond Postgate in his

[1] List and Index Society's volumes 21, 48 and 55 are Department of Education and Science Class Lists; volume 39 is Home Office Registered Papers (H.O. 45), 1920-2, continued in volume 50 for 1923-31 (Part I). Volume 59 is the first part of a list of Ministry of Public Building and Works papers covering 1906-56.

life of George Lansbury. After Lansbury's death in 1940 (he had been First Commissioner of Works in 1929–31) the Cabinet Office demanded the return of papers marked 'Secret'. Reluctantly his biographer and son-in-law, Raymond Postgate, handed over some thirty boxes of official papers on the understanding that the 'Secret' ones would be taken out—'a dozen at most a score', the Treasury Solicitor had said—and the rest returned. Postgate had been unable to sort or examine the papers during the war, which was still raging. The Cabinet Office seized the lot, returning, as a sorry joke, only some applications to subscribe to the *Labour Gazette* in 1893.[1] Such tactics had somewhat less success against Lloyd George. After he had published his *War Memoirs*, Lloyd George was asked by the Cabinet Office to return all his archives. He and Churchill consulted together and decided to refuse, judging that the government would not risk a scandal over it. But after Lloyd George's death in 1945 the request was renewed, and his widow agreed to a compromise by which the more important documents were returned.[2]

None the less, there are large collections of private papers which are of historical value, particularly letters which are essentially of a political or semi-official nature, notes, drafts, diaries and collections of newspaper cuttings. Many of these are still in the hands of the persons themselves, or their families. Several collections have been consulted by historians; of others, selections, particularly from diaries, have been published or are promised for publication. For example, selections from the diaries of Harold Nicolson and Thomas Jones, to be considered later, have been published; and a book has been made from the papers of Lord Davidson (J. C. C. Davidson), Baldwin's friend who was Chancellor of the Duchy of

[1] R. Postgate, *Life of George Lansbury* (London, 1951), vii–ix.
[2] B. H. Liddell Hart, *Memoirs* Vol. I (London, 1965), 369–70. See below p. 111. Lansbury and Churchill had corresponded in 1934, evidently at the time of a previous demand for the return of papers. The two men had agreed for themselves and their heirs that the demand was illegal and it had not been pressed. The Labour Cabinet had resolved in 1931 that ministers were entitled to retain their papers, as they were the property of the government *of the day*, not of the Crown (Postgate, loc. cit.).

Lancaster in 1923 and 1931–7.[1] One of the largest and richest collections of private papers, if they can be called that, is the Royal Archives at Windsor. Several recent historians have been allowed to draw on its resources.

In tracing collections of documents, whether still in private hands or in libraries or local record offices, the historian can call upon the help of the National Register of Archives. This was created by the government in 1945 as part of the Historical Manuscripts Commission. At its offices in Chancery Lane it keeps a complete set of all the reports it has received of collections of papers; copies of these reports are distributed fairly widely in libraries throughout the country. It also maintains at its offices card indexes of all the collections of which it has reports; these comprise a selective index of persons, a subject index and a topographical index. It publishes annually a List of *Accessions to Repositories* (county record offices and designated public libraries and university libraries). Its *Bulletin*, also published annually, describes the main collections added to repositories.[2] For example, the *Bulletin* for 1964 has notes on collections of trade union records, that for 1967 reports on the archives of the Veteran Car Club and of John Pollitt, a pioneer in the motor industry; it also describes the Pre-nationalisation Archives of the Southern Gas Board. In February 1968 a project was inaugurated for collecting further information about papers of a political character: the Nuffield College Project for the Location and Preservation of Modern British Political Records. Its object is to report on the whereabouts of the papers of all British government ministers, inside or outside the Cabinet, between 1900 and 1951, and to collate this information with that possessed by the National Register of Archives and other sources.[3]

Nowadays many families lack the space or means for keeping

[1] R. R. James, ed., *Memoirs of a Conservative: J. C. C. Davidson's Memoirs and Papers, 1910–1937* (London, 1969).

[2] National Register of Archives leaflet, *Facilities offered to students*, Quality Court, Chancery Lane, London W.C.2.

[3] Association of Contemporary Historians, *Interim Bulletin*, July 1968 (duplicated).

the papers of the dead and are willing to place them in a library on gift or loan, sometimes subject to restrictions such as a fifty-year rule; indeed, if moving house is imminent, this may be the only way for the papers to be preserved rather than destroyed. Sometimes they are bought, as were Lord Russell's papers by McMaster University in Ontario, which earned for the dealers who negotiated the sale a nominal fine. Contemporary historians are now, in fact, as much concerned about the control of the export of historical manuscripts as their brethren who write of earlier times. At present an export licence is needed for the export of manuscripts over a hundred years old; the system, dating back to 1940, has several loopholes, and does not in general apply to papers or collections worth less than £50. Unwillingness to interfere with the legitimate business of the antiquarian book-dealers has, not unnaturally, prevented any stringent regulations to retain important collections in Great Britain. A bill to remedy this condition of affairs was introduced by Mr David Marquand, M.P., in 1969, and the government promised to give the problem serious consideration. The bill would require an export licence for the export of manuscripts of historical importance of whatever age; provide for Xerox copying of manuscripts whose export is permitted; for delay so that manuscripts at risk may be purchased for a British library; for the use of archivists and historians to advise about the issue or refusal of licences, and for penalties up to £1,000 fine or one year's imprisonment for infringement of the law.

In fact, a surprisingly large number of private papers are now safely in libraries—university libraries, county record offices, the British Museum. D. C. Watt has given a very useful list in his *Personalities and Policies: Studies in the Formulation of British Foreign Policy in the Twentieth Century* (London, 1965). The British Museum has the papers of Balfour and Viscount Cecil (Lord Robert Cecil) and John Burns, for example. H. A. L. Fisher's papers, Gilbert Murray's, Asquith's are at the Bodleian in Oxford. The Cambridge University Library has the papers of Baldwin, Sir Samuel Hoare and Lord Crewe, all subject to a fifty-year rule. The London School of Economics has the papers of Sidney and

Beatrice Webb, Hugh Dalton, Lansbury, Violet Markham, E. D. Morel. Lord Lothian's papers and Haldane's are in Edinburgh, Austen Chamberlain's at Birmingham University, Thomas Jones' at the National Library of Wales, Aberystwyth. The papers of several naval men are at the National Maritime Museum, of military men (under restricted access) at the Imperial War Museum—where there is also an invaluable collection of war diaries, letters and reminiscences of ordinary soldiers.

The most assiduous collector of statesmen's papers in recent years was Lord Beaverbrook. Apart from his own papers, he acquired those of Lloyd George, Frances Stevenson (Countess Lloyd-George), Bonar Law, Sir Patrick Hannon and Lord Wargrave. These were destined for the University of New Brunswick, a decision which was changed, to the good fortune of historians working in Great Britain. They are now housed in the Beaverbrook Library behind the *Daily Express* building on Fleet Street, where they are in the care of A. J. P. Taylor. The Lloyd George papers had been admirably arranged and catalogued under the direction of Mrs G. R. Elton before the Library was opened, and are easy to consult. It is clear that the Library will become a factory for scholarly studies of Lloyd George and his times.

County record offices, and possibly the libraries of the newer universities, may well come to have more private papers in future. If these treasures remain unknown, it is not the fault of the county archivists, who are most willing to open their collections to responsible researchers—and, indeed, to less responsible seekers, since they are public offices with obligations to all citizens. The guide, *Record Repositories in Great Britain* (H.M. Stationery Office, 3rd edition, 1968) should be consulted.

The papers of political parties and trade unions are dispersed and elusive. Nuffield College has been forming an archive of Labour and trade union papers, partly based on G. D. H. Cole's collection, and has the papers of Herbert Morrison and Jack Tanner (of the Amalgamated Engineering Union) and the diary of G. R. Strauss. Other holdings of trade union and Labour documents exist at the headquarters of the Trades Union Congress and in some trade union offices, at the London School of Economics, Hull University, the Marx Memorial Library. Party headquarters must have archives of some sort—the Communist and Labour parties certainly do; for one reason or another they are not very accessible. Gaps can, however, sometimes be filled from local collections; e.g., records of the local trades council in the public library. But the list of possibilities is almost endless, and there is no substitute for ingenuity and pertinacity in tracking them down.

Perhaps it should be added that access to papers, whether in the government's archives or in a library, does not confer the right to publish material seen or copied or extracts from it, without permission of the owner of the copyright. Copyright usually remains with the writer of any document or his heirs or trustees, and government papers are protected by Crown Copyright.

CHAPTER 4

Memoirs, Diaries and Biographies

Memoirs, Diaries, and Biographies

I. THE BIOGRAPHICAL APPROACH

'Biography is not a good way of writing history,' Professor Elton
has declared; and of course within limits he is right. The biographer's task is to tell the story of a man's life, bringing out his
personality and his importance; 'he should not be concerned with
the history of that individual's times except in so far as it centres
upon or emanates from him.'[1] The qualification is important. For
a great many men who become the subject of biographies it is the
political career (or the career in science or business) which provides
not merely the interest but the *raison d'être* of the biography. The
man's private life may not be particularly interesting (or if interesting may be irrelevant to his public career); his work was his life.
If so, his life cannot be written without telling a great deal about
the times in which he was active: the politics, the party battles,
foreign policy. In so far as his life is written not long after his
lifetime it may provide the first detailed study of a period or
episode in political history. If, as is frequently the case, it quotes
generously from letters, a diary, personal papers, it may open up
important evidence for the historian.

For the recent and contemporary historian the same is true, to a
much greater extent, of published diaries and memoirs. They
provide, at least ostensibly, first-hand information about events,
persons, decisions; the author can make the clinching declaration
'I was there.' Was he? That is a question we must defer. Now we
need only notice that we must consult the writers of memoirs, the
autobiographers and diarists, using what safeguards we can;
because for a while they may be our only 'sources'. They are a
way into the closed period, before the thirty-year rule, or whatever rule is in force, has opened the archives.

[1] Elton, *Practice of History*, 169–70.

Each of these forms of personal record has its pitfalls, but each has something to give the historian under at least one of three headings. It will tell something of the personality of the man, and if he played a part in major events and decisions this may help to explain how things went as they did, or how certain decisions came to be made. We may discount the human factor in the causes of wars and revolutions and innovations, but we cannot banish it altogether. Second, it may help us to understand the mood of the times, the feel of events. Third, a biography or diary or memoirs may establish the facts—a key date, a critical meeting, some inner reasons. True, it may do the contrary, and start a myth or prolong an error: the risk must be taken and can be guarded against. Somewhere along the line, from personal trivia and impressions on the one hand to invaluable historical evidence on the other, any book in the biographical genre may prove helpful to the historian.

How can you tell whether a biography or book of reminiscences does contain information or convey impressions which are of value to the historian? What you get out of any book depends on what you bring to it; the better you know the period or the subject the better you can judge it.

Often, reviewers can be of great help in pointing to important discoveries or refuting false claims. This assumes, however, that the reviewer himself knows his subject. Sometimes he does not, and this can be true of a reviewer in one of the professional historical journals as much as in a newspaper or weekly magazine where the task may be entrusted to a literary man or a political journalist. How can you know your reviewers? Only by *their* books and articles, their reputation. Yet an unknown reviewer may prove to be a sound critic. At this point one can only return to the book itself, and judge it in the light of one's own knowledge, comparing it with other authorities.

One further warning. Biographies, diaries and memoirs form so vast a literature that selections from it must be personal. Omission is no dismissal of a book as worthless; it may result from ignorance or poor judgment. Since we are concerned with types, this is perhaps not as serious a handicap as it might seem.

2. BIOGRAPHIES

The production of biographies (and again we quote Professor Elton) 'forms one of the country's most flourishing industries, and they are well liked by readers'. The industry has not yet, however, entered the market for lives of the great ones of the twentieth century in a big way. Perhaps it is the lack of available private papers, perhaps it is the old fifty-year rule, perhaps simply that there are no earlier biographies to pillage or correct or outdo. At the risk of being thought too exclusive we might say that there have been only five or six major biographies of weight and substance which *of themselves* illuminate some part of British history since 1914.[1]

Robert Blake's *Unknown Prime Minister: The Life and Times of Andrew Bonar Law* (London, 1955) is the first. It is solidly based on Bonar Law's papers, and on a host of memoirs. Much of it, of course, deals with Bonar Law's career before 1914, including his election as leader of the Conservative Party and his violent in-fighting and support for the rebels in the struggle to save Ulster from incorporation in a Home-Rule Ireland. After 1914 Bonar Law's role in affairs was much more central, and Blake has demonstrated this to great effect and with a wealth of detail. His part in the formation of Asquith's coalition in 1915, in Lloyd George's move to the War Office in 1916, in the crisis of December 1916 when Bonar Law's support, against the wishes of several of his leading Conservative colleagues, was vital to Lloyd George's move to the prime ministership, in the War Cabinet, and in both complementing and countering Lloyd George's abilities in a strange and effective partnership from 1916 to 1921—all this was made clear only when Mr Blake's work was published. And on two episodes at least the new evidence brought by Mr Blake was decisive in replacing the accepted version by a new one. It became

[1] Perhaps I should add the life of Baldwin published since I wrote these lines: R. K. Middlemas and J. Barnes, *Baldwin* (London, 1969). Unfortunately its great length and the obscurity of its system of reference may discourage readers from getting the best out of it.

clear that it was Bonar Law's voice, not Baldwin's, which was decisive at the Carlton Club meeting in October 1922. And for the first time the full, strange story of how Baldwin rather than Curzon became Prime Minister in 1923 was told. Bonar Law intimated that he preferred not to advise the King about his successor. However, the truth is sometimes established bit by bit, as more evidence is accumulated. Thomas Jones' *Whitehall Diary*, and Lord Davidson's memoirs, published in 1969, have since added evidence that Baldwin would have been Bonar Law's recommendation if the King had asked him. As it was, Sir Ronald Waterhouse, his private secretary, gave the King's private secretary, Lord Stamfordham, a memorandum written by J. C. C. Davidson (as he was then), arguing the case for Baldwin. It was a natural inference that it represented Bonar Law's views; in fact he did not know of it.[1]

Very different was the hero of Alan Bullock's *Life and Times of Ernest Bevin* (London, 1960), of which two volumes have so far appeared, describing Bevin's career to the end of the Second World War. This is a pioneering work in more ways than one; no other trade union leader has been the subject of such a massive and scholarly work. From Bevin's early days among the Bristol dockers to his work as the maker and leader of the Transport and General Workers' Union and a dominating figure in the T.U.C. and the Labour Party between the wars, and then to his achievement as Minister of Labour and National Service in the Churchill coalition, the account is authoritative, the perspective clear. It is Bevin and his times, as seen from trade union headquarters and documented from papers, jottings, stenographic reports, minutes of innumerable committees, both trade union and governmental. It is this documentation which gives the work authority. It can be seen, for instance, in the details of Bevin's plan for a last-minute solution of the coal strike before the government-T.U.C. negotiations to avert the General Strike were broken off. The

[1] R. Blake, *The Unknown Prime Minister* (London, 1955), 516–27; Thomas Jones, *Whitehall Diary*, Vol. I, *1916–1925*, ed. R. K. Middlemas (Oxford, 1969), 236. See below, pp. 101 ff.

work's chief deficiency is that it remains so far incomplete: but no doubt this will be remedied in time.

The life of Neville Chamberlain was written within a few years of his death. Sir Keith Feiling's *Life of Neville Chamberlain* was published in 1946 and it remains not only the standard life but the only major political biography that we have of any of the prime ministers since Bonar Law. It is, perhaps, not a great biography; its language is frequently stilted, its expressions so convoluted as to defeat grammar if not the sense of the passage. But it has scale, and (more important to the student) it has documentation which no later biographer, whatever the secrets revealed in the government papers, will be able to ignore; Chamberlain's diary and his regular letters, a weekly political commentary in effect, to his two sisters. There is, for instance, a full account of Chamberlain's meeting with Hitler at Berchtesgaden, which is much more lively than Chamberlain's fuller account printed in *Documents on British Foreign Policy*; one feels almost as if one was there.[1] Both sources are generously quoted—not necessarily to Chamberlain's advantage, for his ideas, and their excessive simplicity, and his tactics, and their ruthless deviousness, are revealed in his own words. In June 1936, when Chancellor of the Exchequer, he took it upon himself to make the first move to change the British policy of maintaining sanctions, admittedly ineffective, against Italy after the conquest of Abyssinia, declaring in a speech that the policy was 'the very midsummer of madness'. In his diary, quoted by Feiling, he wrote:

I did it deliberately because I felt that the party and the country needed a lead . . . I did not consult Anthony Eden [Foreign Secretary] because he would have been bound to beg me not to say what I proposed . . . He himself has been as nice as possible about it . . . [2]

He practised, and admitted to, a similar deception when he acted without Eden (still the Foreign Secretary) in attempting to initiate conversations with Mussolini, an action which led up to Eden's

[1] K. Feiling, *Life of Neville Chamberlain*, 366–8; see above, p. 46.
[2] *Ibid.*, 296.

resignation in February 1938.[1] And was it naivety or cynicism that caused him to write in November 1937, 'I don't see why we shouldn't say to Germany, "give us satisfactory assurances that you won't use force to deal with the Austrians and Czechoslovakians, and we will give you similar assurances that we won't use force to prevent the changes you want, if you can get them by peaceful means".'[2] It all depends, of course, on what you mean by force, or 'peaceful means'. Since Feiling attempts no whitewashing, his book, with all its weaknesses, has the first quality one seeks in recent biography: an impartiality which reveals defects as well as virtues in the subject.

Another life on a large scale, also still unfinished, is Michael Foot's *Aneurin Bevan* (London, 1962), of which the first volume comes down to 1945. It may be that this is not a great biography, but only a provisional one. It quotes from other biographies and memoirs, from Bevan's writings and his speeches in Parliament. The author has three great advantages. He knew Bevan well, and lived through the same times. He has pursued a political career, shared Bevan's views, and been a member of parliament for many years. He can write about Bevan's political life with authority. This is not to say that no historian can write good political biography unless he himself has got into Parliament; but to have taken some part in public affairs, as Gibbon said long ago, is not unuseful to the historian. But, of course, these advantages have their reverse side. Sharing Bevan's life and work so much, Foot naturally became somewhat identified with him. He is too competent a biographer to overplay the hero-worship, but he cannot be expected to be coolly critical, to see the other point of view, or to assess Bevan's place in contemporary history with dispassion. Biography of this kind has the virtues and defects of the old saints' lives: it tells us much personal and inner detail that would otherwise be lost, but it consistently turns the hero's face to the sun. If there were shadows, they will have to be described by another hand. Saints' lives make better reading than extended

[1] K. Feiling, *Life of Neville Chamberlain*, 330.
[2] *Ibid.*, 333.

articles from a biographical dictionary (like Feiling's *Chamberlain*) but they need more careful criticism. However, Foot's *Bevan* does provide the correction to another saint's life: he writes fully and in considerable detail, and particularly of the war years, when Bevan was a sort of one-man opposition to Churchill, to Bevin, even to the whole coalition. This is a side of the war's history which so far has not been much written about.[1]

We expect royal lives to be massive, esoteric, discreet, the crown more important than the man. Harold Nicolson's *King George V: His Life and Reign* (London, 1952) inaugurated a new style in official lives, and thanks to his published *Diary* we know how the book came to be written. This, exceptionally, provides a ready-made tool of criticism, and the book comes out extremely well. It was written on the invitation of King George VI, and he and other members of the royal family read it in draft. They made very few suggestions of changes. He was given all the papers: 'the idea is that I shall be shown every scrap of paper that exists. I would have a table of my own in the library at Windsor and go down there three days a week.' He was told that he was not expected to write one word that was untrue, but 'must omit things and incidents which were discreditable'.[2] This, indeed, is the only thing in his account of the writing of the book which raises doubts; he does not mention, later in his diary, any suppressions, and the whole tone of the book suggests, what was surely true, that there was nothing to suppress.[3] Work on the book took him three years in all: three years which he devoted to *George V* without abandoning his weekly articles, his gardening at Sissinghurst, and the calls of a busy social life. This is an achievement to put most professional historians to shame; and he had no research assistants, no team of helpers. He made a point of talking with people who had known the King: Queen Mary, Sir Clive Wigram, Lord Cromer and many others. He wrote first the

[1] But see Angus Calder, *The People's War* (London, 1961).
[2] Harold Nicolson, *Diaries and Letters 1945–1962*, ed. N. Nicolson (London, 1968), 142–3.
[3] *Ibid.*, 184.

chapter on the 1931 crisis, so that he could have it checked by people who took part: he had a long talk with Herbert Morrison (Minister of Transport and member of the Cabinet at the time), who gave him a note of his reminiscences. In fact he has given us a model for writing a life of a contemporary figure: interviews with survivors, and access to—in this case—full and beautifully kept archives.[1]

The results can be seen in *King George V*, one of the great biographies of the century. Not only is the human side of the King shown to the full—with the help of his diaries—but equal justice is done to his role as a constitutional monarch who remained entitled to advise and to warn his ministers. The King's skill and wisdom was much tested from the first, in the 'constitutional crisis' over the Parliament Bill in 1910–11 and the Ulster crisis of 1912–14. Later, his conciliation was employed in the crisis caused by Asquith's resignation in December 1916; the King summoned a conference of senior ministers, including Asquith, to discuss who should form a government. How far the crown retains any power of independent action, to refuse a dissolution, which was in question in 1916, 1923 and 1924, or to assist in the choice of prime minister, as in 1931, is discussed with the authority of the papers in the Royal Archives, particularly of the King's private secretaries, Lord Stamfordham and Sir Clive Wigram. Indeed, the high importance of that discreet office was first fully revealed in this book. The King's role as King of each dominion in the evolving Commonwealth is also explored; it was tested in the appointment of a new governor-general for Australia in 1930. One notices also the King's interventions with the government behind the scenes, always in the cause of sanity and moderation, at the time of the General Strike; or again one admires the tactful handling of Sir Douglas Haig, who as commander-in-chief was in 1917 writing private letters from France to the King. This biography has forced the historian to revise the inherited virtue of the age from which the King was effectively absent.

[1] Harold Nicolson, *Diaries and Letters 1945–1962*, ed. N. Nicolson (London, 1968), 147, 162, 164, 166–8, 175–6, 191–2, 209 and *passim*.

Last, a distinguished biography of a man who was not directly in politics, J. M. Keynes the economist. Sir Roy Harrod's *Life of John Maynard Keynes* (London, 1951) is on a generous scale and illuminates much beside the man: the circle of friends at Cambridge which grew into the Bloomsbury set, the Treasury and the Paris Peace Conference, depression and Liberal thinking about economics in the twenties, the evolution of Keynes' contributions to economic theory, government and finance in the Second World War, the Bretton Woods negotiations which preceded the making of the International Monetary Fund, and the negotiation of the 1946 American loan to Britain. The sources are a great range of private letters and papers of Keynes and his friends, and personal information in interview or correspondence from a host of Keynes' contemporaries. At the same time, it is hard to avoid an impression, once again, that a touch of hagiography (modern style) has entered the treatment. Since the book appeared, some aspects of Keynes's private life have become public; more important, his authority as an economist, still overwhelming, has become less absolutely unchallengeable. Harrod wrote as a friend (enemies do not write good biographies), and the reader needs to be aware of this. At the same time, the problem of assessing the book and its subject underlines the problems of very recent biography: it is bound to be overtaken by the development of knowledge and needs to be revised critically at intervals.

It may be misleading to dismiss biographies as sources after selecting a mere half dozen for distinction. Any life must tell something of the man and his theme, and almost any life will make use of private papers which would otherwise remain unknown. Occasionally, a series of studies will interlock sufficiently to correct biases or fill a gap. A good example is found in the strange history of a group of men who worked together very cohesively and on the whole rather overestimated their own influence on affairs, a misjudgment shared by contemporaries and to some extent by their biographer. There is much to be learned about Lloyd George's War Cabinet and the early years of the post-war Coalition from A. M. Gollin's *Proconsul in Politics: a*

Study of Lord Milner in Opposition and in Power (London, 1964), which is soundly based on the sources and quotes extensively from them. Milner was a very odd fish, and his racial ideas, his scorn of parliamentary democracy, his fury against Asquith's government and Home Rule, his shrill cries for violence (from his armchair) in defence of Ulster are not pleasing. But he was a loyal and invaluable member of the War Cabinet, trusted by Lloyd George and trusting him in turn to a degree not recognised until Gollin's study appeared. Moreover, it is only through biographical works of this kind that one can learn something of that curious sect of ambitious wire-pullers, Milner's 'kindergarten', which tried to steer British policy from behind the scenes in the 1920s and 1930s, working on influential public opinion (i.e., *The Times*, the Athenaeum, All Souls[1]) for the cause of the Commonwealth idea and, latterly, the appeasement of Hitler. It contributed to the 'Cliveden set', though the Astors' friends were very much more widespread; its influence can easily be exaggerated but it cannot be ignored. It can be studied in J. R. M. Butler's life of Lord Lothian (1960) and Evelyn Wrench's life of *Geoffrey Dawson and Our Times* (London, 1955); the latter must be checked against the *History of the Times*, Vol. IV, Part 2 (1952) which, written after the war, was highly critical of Dawson's policies in the thirties. Between them, all these books make possible a reasonably accurate judgment where singly they often mislead.

Another source, at first blush an unlikely one, for the political history of the period is the *Lives of the Lord Chancellors 1885–1940* by R. F. V. Heuston (Oxford, 1964). This continuation of Atlay's *Victorian Chancellors* includes the holders of the office from Lord Halsbury to Lord Caldecote (Sir Thomas Inskip), but it is no mere lawyer's study of lawyers. Professor Heuston has dug into the papers of successive chancellors and their colleagues and quoted freely from them. The result is to remind one that public life made strange bed-fellows, and that one is wise to attempt an exhaustive coverage of the evidence even in unpromising circumstances. For example, from the papers of Ernest Pollock, the

[1] See A. L. Rowse's *caveat, All Souls and Appeasement* (London, 1961).

Attorney-General, Heuston tells of a deputation of leading Conservatives to Austen Chamberlain in June 1922 to express concern over the 'sale of honours', and of a second meeting on 3 August at which Lord Birkenhead, the Lord Chancellor, berated the critics, and Pollock in particular, in strong terms: 'our whole conduct was a compound of insubordination and stupidity'. Birkenhead's behaviour undoubtedly contributed to Conservative distrust of the Coalition, ending in the Carlton Club meeting; a last attempt to win Chamberlain away from the Coalition two days beforehand also failed.[1] From Lord Hailsham's papers we get some examples of Baldwin's brief, chirpy letters, and of Baldwin's own brand of higher selfishness; a letter of 4 August 1928 virtually ordering Hailsham to forgo his holiday in Canada and act as Baldwin's deputy so that Baldwin could have his usual six weeks' holiday at Aix. 'If I could get away later,' Baldwin wrote, 'I would stay myself now, but my holiday is strictly bound by the Yarmouth Conference of September 27th, and unless I can get a good holiday before that I should be unfit for the strain of the coming year with the General Election.'[2] Hailsham obediently abandoned his holiday.

Caldecote's papers are particularly rewarding for Neville Chamberlain's relations with one who, on the face of it, was a close colleague. Inskip was one of the few ministers whom Chamberlain approached about his proposal to visit Hitler (Plan 'Z'): this was on 7 September, a week before Chamberlain sprang the plan on the whole Cabinet (which had also met on the 12th). The others consulted in advance were Halifax, Simon, Kingsley Wood and 'I think also Malcolm MacDonald'. At the Cabinet on the 14th Walter Elliot complained of not having been consulted, and so having difficulty in approving or disapproving of the plan; the rest of the Cabinet supported it. When Chamberlain returned from Berchtesgaden and reported to the Cabinet on the 19th, Inskip's account is realistic and unadmiring:

[1] R. F. V. Heuston, *Lives of the Chancellors*, 387–9.
[2] *Ibid.*, 472.

The impression made by the P.M.'s story was a little painful. Hitler had made him listen to a boast that the German military machine was a terrible instrument, ready to move now, and once put in motion could not be stopped. The P.M. said more than once to us that he was just in time. It was plain that Hitler had made all the running: he had in fact blackmailed the P.M.

Opposition to accepting Hitler's demands upon Czechoslovakia came from Duff Cooper, Oliver Stanley and Lord Winterton, though all ultimately assented.[1] A few months later, in January 1939, Inskip recorded a rather unpleasant interview in which Chamberlain suddenly unfolded his plan of moving him from the post of Minister for the Co-ordination of Defence. After a long lead-in—he proposed to give Inskip the Dominions Office—Chamberlain continued:

> Then the question comes who will take your place. I can't put a junior Minister in the position, and I can't see anyone in the Cabinet that will do the job as well as you have done it. I can only think of one man.
>> (I rapidly thought—or tried to think—of someone, but I failed, and neither Anthony Eden nor Winston came into my mind.)
> P.M.: I propose Chatfield [Admiral of the Fleet].
>> (My mouth opened, or my eyes.)
> P.M.: I know what you are going to say: 'He belongs to one of the Services.'
>> (I wasn't going to say this. I was thinking of his position in the House of Lords.)
> But I think he can hold the scales; he has been out of the Admiralty for some time now, and I think he will give the public confidence . . .

Chamberlain explained that he thought Inskip should stay in the House of Commons, to 'keep open—if you like—your chance of being P.M.'. This, which will strike historians as grotesque, was a view of Inskip's capacity which others shared, as is shown by a letter from the Duke of Devonshire after his death, which Heuston quotes (p. 601). In the end Inskip asked if the Dominions would feel they were being fobbed off with a failure.

[1] R. F. V. Heuston, *Lives of the Chancellors*, 591–3.

P.M.: I am sure they will not. They were delighted to get Malcolm. They didn't know who they might get.

(I thought this was an odd statement if it was intended to reassure me.)

I: Well, if you think it best, of course I am in your hands.[1]

No wonder that when, on the outbreak of war in September, Chamberlain told Inskip that he wanted to make a change at the Dominions Office, giving no reason but offering him the Lord Chancellorship, he commented, 'I don't like the P.M.'s methods. He is a "faux ami", and I think I shall be glad to be out of his inner circle.'[2] This is not the Chamberlain—or the Inskip—of public memory, a necessary reminder of the value of improbable sources.

It remains only to ask, before we leave the biographies, why there have not been major lives of the major politicians. Lloyd George has attracted several biographers: one of his secretaries, Malcolm Thomson, Frank Owen, a journalist, Thomas Jones of the Cabinet Office, his renegade son Richard who first put into print the stories of his father's marital infidelities. Frank Owen's book is the longest, and the introduction claimed that the author had gone through 1,025 boxes of papers and more than two hundred books in writing it. And there are some useful quotations from the papers; but there is no grasp of the man, and the breathless tone and the contrived dramatic effects do not make up for the lack of judgment and proportion. Tom Jones' book is the best, understanding but not uncritical; its only shortcoming is its brevity. With Lloyd George the present question is whether he has been unfortunate in his biographers or simply cannot be captured on paper. Either way, the gap in contemporary history is serious. Of the other prime ministers between the wars Mac-Donald was to have been written of by his son Malcolm, and when the duties of office prevented this the family entrusted the task to David Marquand; its discharge has evidently been slowed up by his election to Parliament. Baldwin has had an odd fate. His

[1] *Ibid.*, 595–6.
[2] *Ibid.*, 600.

chosen biographer, G. M. Young, evidently came to dislike the task, and in his very short life actually joined Baldwin's critics in discussing his record on defence and foreign policy in the thirties, while making excessive claims for him in other directions. D. C. Somervell leapt to Baldwin's defence in a short reply (1953), which only made matters worse.[1] The best book at present is by his son, A. W. Baldwin, *My Father: the True Story* (London, 1955), which is an exception to the rule that one cannot trust filial biographers to be balanced and fair-minded. The long-promised life, which was even announced in advance as 'definitive'—surely a title that can only be conferred by the judgment of responsible critics after publication?—by John Barnes and R. K. Middlemas, has now made massive amends.[2]

The official life of Winston Churchill, begun by Randolph Churchill and to be completed by Martin Gilbert, has not yet reached the First World War.

3. DIARIES

Of twentieth-century diaries it may be said that if many have been kept, few have been published. One of the earliest was Christopher (later Lord) Addison's *Four and a Half Years* which appeared in two volumes in 1934 and covers the period June 1914 to January 1919. It has never had much attention, and is not perhaps the most exciting reading, but as a day-by-day account of the war years it deserves to be used. Addison, a Liberal, was close to Lloyd George, and gives many impressions of him, his working breakfasts (as they would now be called), his methods and intuitions. Addison went with Lloyd George to the new Ministry of Munitions, and succeeded him there, later taking over the Ministry of Reconstruction. He was the leading spirit in marshalling the Liberals (the later 'Coalies' so despised by Asquith's supporters, the 'Squiffites') behind Lloyd George in 1916.

[1] See my review article, 'Baldwin Restored?' in *Journal of Modern History*, XXVII, 169–74 (June 1955).

[2] See above, p. 87.

How reliable are diaries as sources? One needs to know whether a diary was written up each day, or only days later; one needs to know something of the diarist's memory, his powers of observation and recall. One needs to know if the entries in the diary have been altered when hindsight changed an impression or an incident. One needs to know, perhaps, whether the diarist had any intention of publishing the diary at the time of writing it. Where the published version is the work of an editor we can judge the authenticity of the text by the editor's reputation and the quality of his footnotes, and we must trust his judgment in making selections; for no diary has been published *in extenso*. In any case the cardinal rule applies: the evidence from the diary must if possible be supported by evidence from other sources.

An interesting and unusual demonstration of the use of a diary comes from Sir Arthur Bryant's study of Sir Alan Brooke (Lord Alanbrooke), Chief of the Imperial General Staff under Churchill in the Second World War. After the war, Alanbrooke went through his wartime diaries and added 'notes of comment and amplification'. Sir Arthur Bryant, a historian, was then allowed to write a book whose sub-title explains its character: 'A History of the War Years Based on the Diaries of Field-Marshal Lord Alanbrooke, Chief of the Imperial General Staff'. We thus have three voices, the diary's, sometimes tired and irritated, the emollient commentary, and Sir Arthur Bryant.[1] Alanbrooke's disparaging references to General Eisenhower's lack of tactical and strategical experience, though toned down by the commentary, were resented when the book was published.[2] In fact the book is little different from any other published diary save in the honesty with which its triple voices are separated. An editor is at liberty to exclude passages from a diary if he thinks they will give offence or reflect badly on the diarist; he, or the diarist himself if he is writing his memoirs, is at liberty to add later comment. At any rate, the

[1] Arthur Bryant, *The Turn of the Tide* (London, 1957), 21–22 explains the two voices and gives an example. There is a second volume, *Triumph in the West* (London, 1959).

[2] *Ibid.*, 430; cf. p. 454 where it is Alanbrooke's comment that is disparaging.

book is one of the best accounts of the crosses and joys of working with Churchill, his fits of temper and rudeness, his gusto and kindliness, the appalling hours he put his staff to—up to 2 a.m. or 3 a.m., and then ready to start work again at breakfast

The most uninhibited diary to be published is that of an earlier general, Sir Henry Wilson, a political general if ever there was one, though his contempt for the politicians (the 'frocks' as he called them) was great.[1] He was a chronic meddler, whose leaks of War Office plans to the Conservative Opposition during the Ulster crisis of 1912–14 (he was a fanatical Ulsterman) bordered on treason. Lloyd George had a high opinion of him, and made him C.I.G.S. in succession to Sir William Robertson. His advice on the Black and Tan war in Ireland in 1920–1 was harsh if realistic; he objected to the government's condoning of 'unofficial' reprisals, and in 1921 told the government, shortly before the truce, that the choice was 'to go all out or to get out'. Wilson was a freak among the generals, and perhaps his diary should not be taken too seriously. But 'he was there', and he was not without influence.

Much better known are Beatrice Webb's diaries, of which two selections were published after her death: *Diaries 1912–1924* in 1952, and *1924–1932* in 1956, edited by Margaret Cole. These carried on the work done by Mrs Webb herself in writing *My Apprenticeship* (London, 1926) and *Our Partnership* (London, 1948) covering the years from her marriage in 1892 until 1911. Both books, the latter published posthumously, were made up largely of extracts from the diaries put together by Mrs Webb, with connecting commentaries, as she worked through them. She was engaged in this task intermittently from 1926 to her death. Her editor, in publishing the later diaries, followed her method of choosing extracts, but without attempting anything in the way of commentary. They will long be the source for rather waspish judgments on Labour colleagues and friends and acquaintances. They record the gossip that reached the partnership at 41

[1] C. E. Callwell, *Field-Marshal Sir Henry Wilson, His Life and Diaries* (2 vols., London, 1927).

Grosvenor Road or Passfield Corner, and the impressions of a wayward, astringent mind well-armed with preconceptions. Yet the Webbs' influence was pervasive, and the diaries' evidence of it and of their ways of thinking remains important. Sidney Webb was in both the Labour governments (1924 and 1929), so that the diaries are a source for them, more perhaps for their flavour and personalities than for their inner history. There is, however, a useful grain of information about the Zinoviev Letter. The trouble about selecting any of the innumerable character sketches for quotation is that they are nearly always long, and their spirit is lost by abbreviation. One of the many on Ramsay MacDonald must suffice:

> . . . it hurts my pride to see the Fabian policy of permeation 'guyed' by MacDonald. Yet as a political performer he is showing himself a consummate artist. We had never realised that he had genius in this direction.[1] (15 March 1924)

The most assiduous diarist of the times was Thomas Jones, the Welsh miner's son who became a professor of economics and joined the Cabinet Secretariat as one of its first recruits in December 1916 after being summoned to London by Lloyd George to help concert the plan which matured into Lloyd George's War Cabinet. He remained in the Cabinet Office, as deputy secretary, until he retired in 1930. He kept a diary from December 1916 onwards. The annual volumes were printed privately in a few copies in Switzerland and stored in various places. 'T.J.' selected large parts of them for the years after his retirement and published them, together with letters to and from himself, as *A Diary with Letters 1931–1950* in 1954; the bulk of the book is concerned with the years 1931–40. His lengthy introduction, 'Of Prime Ministers, Private Secretaries, Hostesses, and Clubs' was intended to be an introduction to all his diaries, and includes his inside view of the Cabinet Office, of Hankey, 'the prince of secretaries', and of the private secretary's character, 'a passion for anonymity and secret

[1] *Beatrice Webb's Diaries 1924–1932*, 14.

influence' (attributes T.J. possessed in full, save that he was by no means anonymous, nor wished to be, in a large circle of men and women in politics, society and education). This introduction contains admirable character sketches of his Prime Ministers, Lloyd George, Bonar Law, Baldwin and MacDonald, with all of whom, except MacDonald, he was on terms of intimacy. He also analyses the Cliveden set, for he was a very frequent visitor to the Astors at Cliveden, pointing out its catholicity, that Neville Chamberlain was down there for week-ends only five times in the years 1930–9, that it was largely a place for talk, 'a comfortable theatre for the conversational interplay of political personalities. The talk was always of the problems which exercised Parliament, Whitehall, the Foreign Office, the Empire, France, Germany, America; everlastingly of the rise and fall of Parties and leaders and reputations, the competents and the disappointments.'[1] (Cliveden tipped Walter Elliot as a future prime minister.) Such talk, we might think, is not as innocent as it sounds, since it may give or confirm ideas in those who have power to carry them out.

None the less, *A Diary with Letters* is a prime source. Here one can see what an insider, with no official position, heard and said and thought during ten critical years. There is much, for instance, on Edward VIII's abdication. There is his account of Lloyd George's visit to Hitler in 1936, which he attended (he tried to promote a meeting between Hitler and Baldwin). Throughout these years he was very close to Baldwin, dropping in to see him almost daily in London, and helping to write his speeches. No historian can ignore this first-hand record of a privileged observer, however much he may suspect some of the gossip. That there was such gossip is a fact of importance.

Now selections from the earlier diaries are being published in three volumes, of which the first two, *Whitehall Diary*, Vol. I, *1916–1925*, and Vol. II, *1926–1930*, appeared in 1969, edited by R. K. Middlemas. The first volume has only fairly brief passages on Ireland, with whose affairs T.J. was much concerned: Ireland is to have a separate volume. The editor explains his methods, and

[1] T. Jones, *Diary with Letters*, xxxix.

his grounds for selection and exclusion (matters personal or of specialised interest or extraneous to the main theme); he, like T.J. in *A Diary with Letters*, gives us about one-sixth of the whole diaries. As far as one can judge, the editor has done his work conscientiously, though the biographical footnotes and some other notes are unreliable. He has followed a recent bad practice of annotating perfectly well-known persons: the obscure, of whom one would welcome some identification, get nothing. But no one should take biographical footnotes for the truth, let alone the whole truth, without verification.

T.J. was no ordinary civil servant, and the Cabinet Secretariat in his day was not what it became later. Cabinet meetings and reports were fuller, as we have already seen; even so, T.J.'s reports given here, sometimes with conversation quoted verbatim, are fuller than the official ones, as is shown in parallel extracts from a meeting of the Cabinet's Irish Committee on 9 May 1918.[1] No Cabinet secretary today would keep confidential minutes of his own; nor would he, as T.J. did, help to write political speeches, including some for use in election campaigns.

What can we learn from *Whitehall Diary*? More impressions of Lloyd George, Bonar Law, Baldwin and many other people. More of the working of the Cabinet Office, and of the services of T.J. himself. More about the events of the political crisis of December 1916 and its aftermath. There is a new account—not that it changes the essence of the story—of the 'doormat' incident in which Arthur Henderson left the Cabinet in August 1917. There are three pages of dialogue in the Cabinet on 15 October 1918 when the negotiations with President Wilson over armistice terms to Germany were being discussed. It ended thus:

A. J. B[alfour]: His [Wilson's] style is most inaccurate. He's a first-rate rhetorician and a very bad draftsman.
Reading: What do you expect from a man who typewrites his message in his little room without consulting anyone?[1]

[1] T. Jones, *Whitehall Diary*, I, 62–4.
[2] *Ibid.*, 70.

On 2 February 1920 there was a long 'conference' of ministers on industrial unrest, of which we are given a four-page report. T.J.'s comment at the end is a warning to the researcher not to take these conferences too literally: 'throughout the discussion the P.M. did a lot of unsuspected leg-pulling, as he does not believe in the imminence of the revolution and more than suspects the War Office of trying to increase the army on these lines.'[1] There is another long verbatim report (thirteen pages) of Cabinet discussions on the coal strike just before 'Black Friday' in 1921.[2] There is a great deal on the Campbell case and the Zinoviev Letter in 1924.

Last, there are Harold Nicolson's diaries, unique because they are the record of a man of letters who moved in high society and at the same time pursued a somewhat frustrated political career. Again, what we have are selections made by his son, but even selections fill three volumes, covering the years 1930–62. The diary was begun when Harold Nicolson resigned from the Foreign Service, at the age of forty-three. It was typed by him, usually after breakfast; sometimes at times of pressure it was dictated. It was not written, so Nicolson declared in 1964 when its publication was discussed, with the intention of publishing; and indeed one must say that parts of it, revealing his quest for a peerage, his ambiguity, even opportunism, in joining the Labour Party after the war, his attitude to dull or common people so easily mistaken for snobbishness, put a blemish on the character of a man who was essentially urbane and sincere. It is by all odds the most pleasurable of modern diaries to read. Much of it is personal: his love for his wife, the novelist V. Sackville-West, in a strange but intensely happy marriage, their work together in rescuing a house and creating the garden at Sissinghurst Castle in Kent, and his accounts of luncheons and dinners, parties given by Emerald (Cunard) and Sibyl (Colefax) and other hostesses of the day. Letters of H.N. to V.S-W., as they are referred to, and hers to him, supplement the diaries. His political career sprang from his friendship with 'Tom'

[1] T. Jones, *Whitehall Diary*, I, 103.
[2] *Ibid.*, 132–44.

(Sir Oswald) Mosley, whose New Party he joined in 1931, leaving when Mosley's fascist tendencies became apparent. He was elected to Parliament for Leicester in 1935, as National Labour, member of the phantom party gathered round Ramsay MacDonald and his son Malcolm. He lost his seat in 1945.

Much of the value of the diary is in conveying atmosphere: the feeling of the time of the re-militarisation of the Rhineland by Germany in 1936, of the Abdication crisis, above all of the two weeks' agony ending at Munich, when Nicolson was one of the small group of dissident Conservatives (he refused to cheer when Chamberlain made his dramatic announcement of the invitation to Munich at the end of his speech in Parliament on 28 September). About 'Munich' the diary is particularly full and valuable. There are also sketches of Lloyd George: note how much a diary can add to *Hansard* when Nicolson describes Lloyd George's speech on Austen Chamberlain's death, recalling Gladstone's congratulations to Joseph Chamberlain on Austen's maiden speech, and pointing 'his pince-nez at the place in the House where the protagonists of that sentimental drama were sitting at the time'.[1] There are other impressions and conversations of Lloyd George, of Baldwin, of Ramsay MacDonald, lonely, vain, histrionic, fraudulent yet with a 'core of real simplicity' as Nicolson describes him, and able to make a joke against himself.[2] For the war years the diary's value is perhaps greater, for the day-by-day impressions of a sensitive man in the long, dragging years convey feelings not always remembered. It is also useful to have accounts and commentaries on the wartime debates in the Commons, which were not always plain sailing for Churchill. The debate which preceded Chamberlain's resignation was historic indeed; Nicolson was one of a dissident group acting with another group under Clement Davies, a Liberal member. There are many passages about de Gaulle in London. A Churchillian working week-end at Ditchley is described.[3] And no-one has better described Churchill

[1] Harold Nicolson, *Diaries and Letters 1930–1939* (London, 1966), 296.
[2] *Ibid.*, 67–8, 227, 300.
[3] *Ibid.*, *1939–1945* (London, 1967), 128–9.

as a speaker in the House of Commons, and especially the gestures by which he illustrated his words:

> He began, as always, in a dull, stuffy manner, reciting dates and chronology, reading slowly from the typescript on the box. But as he progressed he began to enliven his discourse with the familiar quips and gestures. His most characteristic gesture is strange indeed. You know the movement that a man makes when he taps his trouser pockets to see whether he has got his latch-key? Well, Winston pats both trouser pockets and then passes his hands up and down from groin to tummy. It is very strange . . . He referred to Italy. . . . 'The satellite States,' he continued, 'suborned and overawed . . .' and then he raised his arm as if about to deliver the most terrific thunderbolt from his rich armoury of rhetoric, but he dropped his arm suddenly and took off his spectacles, '. . . may perhaps be allowed to work their passage home', he concluded, grinning. It is in this that one finds his mastery of the House. It is the combination of great flights of oratory with sudden swoops into the intimate and conversational. Of all his devices it is the one that never fails.[1]

The third volume is inevitably more subdued.[2] Nicolson's public career had ended in 1945; his attempt to return to Parliament as Labour candidate in the Croydon by-election in 1948 ended in failure. His wife's health declined, and the book ends with her death. The writing of the life of King George the Fifth was his principal achievement in these years. But there are things to be gleaned, particularly on the Suez crisis, seen through the eyes of his son Nigel (editor of the diaries) who was Conservative member for Bournemouth at the time and sacrificed his own political career by opposing Eden and supporting Liberal causes which antagonised his constituents. The mood of the grim year 1947 is caught, and of the post-war years generally. We have no other published diary reaching so near to the present day.

This account of some important diaries has illustrated their usefulness. They always illumine personalities (the diarist's and other

[1] Harold Nicolson, *Diaries and Letters, 1930–1939* (London, 1966), 320–1; cf. 280.

[2] *Ibid.*, *1945–1962* (London, 1968).

people's), and they usually add substantially to the store of information. The main problem concerning them, as with all historical evidence, is their trustworthiness. One can commonly do something to correct the diarist's picture of himself. Thus any reader soon realises that Tom Jones's confident temperament enlarged his sense of self-importance and at times tended to exaggerate his influence, while Harold Nicolson's shrinking temperament and determined frankness about himself leave, unusually, an impression unfair to the man. Opinions on others are harder to assess, and only a solid knowledge of the period derived from other sources can help here. The diarist's political position and ambition, as well as the known views and ambitions of the others, must be ascertained first. Here again Nicolson provides an example of the unusual: his politics and his tastes diverged so much that his reactions became both exceptionally self-conscious and exceptionally determined to be fair. As for the events recorded, the path of wisdom lies in scepticism. Too often a diary entry can be shown to be misleading: X was not there to record, as alleged, or Y to be talked to. Of course, more facts in diaries will turn out to be correct than incorrect, but constant checking is necessary. This ought to be the editor's job, but none of these recent diaries have been technically edited at all. The Alanbrooke Diaries give atmosphere and detail of which the first should be taken on trust (this is how Alanbrooke did feel), while the second should be cross-checked with accounts by Churchill, Hopkins and others (and this should have been done by the editor). Unfortunately, material for checking is sometimes hard to find, especially while so many public and private archives remain inaccessible. Newspapers can help at the crude level of ascertaining basic facts. Reviewers, provided their credentials are known, can help establish the reliability of a diary. But the general rule remains one of caution, the more necessary because diaries *can* obviously offer exceptional things to the historian by way of insight and information. And the particular rule is never to start by reading diaries. It cannot be said too often that books like this cannot be read profitably out of ignorance. You must have some knowledge of the period first, so that you know what to look for. Otherwise you will take for new much that is not, and miss the real additions to knowledge. Here, as elsewhere, reviews ought to be a help.

4. MEMOIRS

The most numerous class of biographical materials is the most hazardous to use. The urge to write one's memoirs or reminiscences seems particularly strong among politicians, and to some extent among civil servants, perhaps as a reaction against a career of official reticence. The task may ease the path from a busy life to the greater leisure of retirement. Or it may be taken up under the probing of some friend, or some stranger historian eager for editorial work; or to make money from the serialised excerpts published in one of the newspapers before the book appears. The number of memoirs, for the twentieth century, is legion. D. C. Watt has compiled a long list (which also includes biographies), broken down into categories: Cabinet members, diplomatists, soldiers, sailors and airmen, foreign diplomatic officers, journalists, civil servants and 'other personalities'. He has increased the usefulness of the list by chronological lists of Cabinet members, ministers and civil servants, italicising those who have written memoirs or been the subject of biographies.[1]

Watt's introductory remarks concerning memoirs deserve repeating. The researcher, as he says, is forced back on memoirs when the government documents are closed (though one must add that this is not the only reason for using them). Their usefulness depends on whether the author prefers 'frankness to discretion', and on his freedom with his own manuscript, since ex-ministers are expected to submit their manuscripts to the Cabinet Office for vetting, and civil servants to the head of their department.[2]

[1] D. C. Watt, *Personalities and Policies*, 234–62. Many memoirs are cited in my *Britain between the Wars*, and also (with short comments) in my *British History since 1926: A select Bibliography* (Historical Association pamphlet, 1960).

[2] Watt, *op. cit.*, 224.

Beyond this are many other hazards to the truth. Most men do not keep diaries, and memory is notoriously given to playing tricks. 'Old men forget', as Duff Cooper entitled his memoirs. Memory becomes less sharp, though often sharper for very remote events in childhood or youth. At best it is difficult to recall events ten, twenty or thirty years ago. Newspaper cuttings, old letters, engagement books, *Hansard* may help to jog or correct the memory; and it is not unknown for a ghost-writer to be employed to 'help' by research into what historians have written of the period. Memory may magnify one's own importance in a given set of circumstances. It may convince the writer that he was present somewhere when he was not, met someone he never met, heard someone say something when he only heard it at second or third hand. It is unlikely, unless one has a gift for anecdote, that one can remember the actual words of a conversation. And in addition to all this there is the natural tendency to embroider and embellish, to point the moral and adorn the tale.

As if this was not bad enough, there are more obstacles to truth in memoirs. There is the wisdom of hindsight: 'I thought at the time', 'I remember saying to so and so. . . .' There is the desire to justify oneself, to put the record straight, perhaps to suppress or shade the dubious or the reprehensible action of years ago. No man is on oath in his memoirs. He is pleading at the bar of posterity, but will not hear the verdict.

It matters also how the memoirs have been written. The case of Lord Alanbrooke's diaries has already been cited. The memoirs of J. C. C. Davidson (Lord Davidson) are a case in point.[1] He kept a very large collection of papers and began to write his memoirs many years ago, and then fell ill. Later he added further recollections in tape-recorded conversations with Mr John Barnes. The material was put in final form, supplemented by many contemporary letters, by a third hand. Thus, as A. J. P. Taylor wrote in reviewing the book, in words which apply *mutatis mutandis* to almost any memoirs:

[1] R. R. James, ed., *Memoirs of a Conservative: J. J. Davidson's Memoirs and Papers, 1910–1937* (London, 1969).

The story has thus gone through a number of hands and has also been influenced by the passage of time. Sometimes, one feels, Lord Davidson gave a particular answer because Mr. Barnes asked a particular question. Sometimes Lord Davidson remembered what he had read in someone else's book rather than what he had himself experienced. No man can recall past events without being affected by what has happened in between.[1]

For one example of how memory may mislead, consider again the crisis in May 1940 when Chamberlain, rebuffed in Parliament in the debate on the Norwegian fiasco, decided to resign and summoned Churchill and Halifax to consult as to whom he should advise the King to send for to form a government. Churchill said nothing, and after two minutes' silence Halifax observed that as a peer he could not lead a government, in war-time, from outside the House of Commons. Yet Chamberlain, many Conservatives and several Labour men expected Halifax to become prime minister. Churchill, in his memoirs, puts this critical interview on 10 May, the day of the German invasion of the Low Countries. A. J. P. Taylor, in a brilliant short paragraph describing these events, has pointed out that this interview occurred on the 9th, and that there was a fourth person present, Margesson, the Conservative whip. It is easy to see how Churchill could have confused the dates of the many meetings on two breathless days of suspense and catastrophe. Leo Amery had given the correct date in his memoirs, published several years after Churchill's volume.[2]

With all these difficulties to contend with, the historian might decide to eschew the use of memoirs altogether. He cannot. They are evidence from the past, evidence from contemporaries. They have life and colour, the feel of the times, the impress of the men

[1] *Observer*, 31 August 1969.

[2] A. J. P. Taylor, *English History 1914–1945*, 473–4; W. S. Churchill, *The Gathering Storm* (London, 1948), 595–8; L. S. Amery, *My Political Life*, Vol. III, *The Unforgiving Years 1929–40* (London, 1955), 370–5. I gave the date as 10 May in *Britain between the Wars*, 654, on Churchill's authority, though noting that Amery put the interview on the 9th. A correction for the paperback edition (1968) was set in type but accidentally not used.

and women who helped to shape events; they can inform and explain, or at least give side-lights, as we put it, in a way that the official records never can. Even the poorest memoirs of the most insignificant person may have some precious grain of fact or light of insight. The contemporary historian must use memoirs, but under the normal safeguards, rigorously enforced: verification, confirmation from other sources, common sense, one's own general knowledge of the history of the time.

Amid the mass of twentieth-century memoirs all we can do is to notice a few, arranging them in groups.

From the politicians of the First World War there have been two major writers of memoirs. The first was Lloyd George. Out of office, and by the 1930s perhaps partly resigned to not holding office again (his bid for return to power in the general election of 1929 had failed), he turned to writing his *War Memoirs*, followed by *The Truth about the Peace Treaties*. Tom Jones has described his method of work, aided by his faithful secretaries and reinforced by the mass of documents which they had retained and arranged for him. He proved to have a gift for writing equal to his gifts of oratory; the *Memoirs* read easily and the points are made with effect. Letters and papers are quoted generously. Of course there is much self-justification, and there are things left unsaid. Sir Basil Liddell Hart, who vetted the *Memoirs* for the Cabinet Office at Hankey's request, has testified to the extraordinary fullness and accuracy of the work, which deviates far less than most memoirs from the evidence and provides solid factual material on all the great decisions.[1]

The other compiler of personal history was Lord Beaverbrook. *Politicians and the War* (London, 1928), his first book, is indispensable for the events leading to Lloyd George's assumption of power in December 1916; Aitken, as he then was, was in a

[1] B. H. Liddell Hart, *Memoirs*, Vol. I (London, 1965), 361. See above, p. 78. See also Tom Jones' criticism of the work: *Lloyd George* (London, 1951), 269–73. We still, however, need a really critical appraisal of this important book by an historian, using the historian's techniques and the new materials now available.

unique position as Bonar Law's confidant and promoter to record
—as indeed he helped to shape—what happened. Much later, he
wrote *Men and Power 1917–1918* (London, 1956), a series of
sketches and appendices, with extensive quotations from Lloyd
George's papers. He followed this by *The Decline and Fall of Lloyd
George* (London, 1963), relating the events of the years 1921–2.
This tells as much of Beaverbrook as it does of Lloyd George; in
pursuit of his vision of the future British Empire Beaverbrook
helped to bring about the fall he describes. The book gives the
best account of the divisions within the Cabinet and the government supporters. Lloyd George was at odds with Churchill and
Birkenhead and Curzon, though a peace was patched up between
them, and they stood together over the Irish negotiations. There
is, incidentally, an amusing side-light on the 'sale of honours'
scandal which hurt Lloyd George both then and in retrospect. It
was not the Conservatives who objected—why should they, since
their party and Lloyd George's political funds split the party
contributions between them? The complaint of Sir George
Younger, head of the Conservative organisation, was that they
were not getting their share of the honours: 'I should never have
grumbled,' he wrote to Bonar Law, 'if we had had half of the
list.' He objected also to Conservatives getting rewards on the
Liberal list: '*there must also be a stop to Freddie poaching our men*' (a
reference to Guest, Lloyd George's whip).[1]

Beaverbrook's posthumous *Abdication of King Edward VIII*
(London, 1966), published by A. J. P. Taylor, adds a few pieces of
information to that much be-written affair, and shows Baldwin's
part in the least favourable light. In all Beaverbrook's writings,
the memoir-writer, personally involved, conflicts with the
historian trying to see things at a proper distance. To some extent,
the very fact that the author achieves so much of his ambition to
be the latter detracts from the independent usefulness of what he
provides in his capacity as the former. These recollections were
processed by an historian before the later historian even got to see
them.

[1] Beaverbrook, *Decline and Fall of Lloyd George* (London, 1963), 243.

The war years of 1914–8 are also recorded by a civil servant, a greater secretary even than Tom Jones: Sir Maurice (later Lord) Hankey. Hankey remained secretary of the Cabinet until his retirement in 1938. He also kept a diary. One cannot escape calling him 'the soul of discretion'; no man in the government service can have known and kept so many secrets during a long life. He did, however, publish (beside his short *Diplomacy by Conference* (London, 1946)) two books based on, but not quoting, his diary, *The Supreme Control at the Paris Peace Conference, 1919* (London, 1963) and *The Supreme Command 1914–1918* (two volumes, London, 1961). The latter deals partly with Hankey's early years —the pre-war years—in the Committee of Imperial Defence, but mainly with the work of the Committee's wartime successors in London and with the Supreme War Council when it was set up at Versailles at the end of December 1917. Gallipoli (Hankey was a convinced 'Easterner') and all the military crises on the Western Front are described from the Whitehall end. There are impressions of the leading characters and none of them—not even Sir William Robertson, 'Wullie', the autocratic, unyielding C.I.G.S.—gets a harsh word. For a commentary on the jungle of wartime committees and cabinets, on the crossings innumerable to France for inter-allied meetings, Hankey cannot be bettered. There are occasional glimpses of the men themselves: Lloyd George chanting Welsh hymns and leading the company into a sing-song of old-fashioned songs at Lord Riddell's house, Bonar Law's 'characteristic remark' at a performance of *La Fille de Madame Angot* in Paris that 'it would be less intolerable if only they would not sing'. And we must never forget his judgment on Lloyd George, a judgment he, if anyone, was qualified to make, and he put it in capitals: THE MAN WHO WON THE WAR. Two other things we should not forget are Hankey's just pride in his achievement and his famous discretion. Both are quite apparent in his memoirs and must be taken into account in their use.

Of other civil servants who have written their memoirs it is worth mentioning P. J. Grigg (Sir James Grigg). He was secretary to successive chancellors of the exchequer from 1921 to 1930, and his reminiscences of his chiefs, and especially of Churchill, are valuable. Later he was permanent head of the War Office, and was made by Churchill (an unusual appointment) Secretary for War in 1942–5. His *Prejudice and Judgment* was published in 1948.

Another civil servant, who was also a League of Nations official and later a professor, was Sir Arthur (Lord) Salter. His *Personality in Politics* (London, 1947) and *Memoirs of a Public Servant* (London, 1961) are worth reading.

Sir Robert (Lord) Vansittart was a Foreign Office man and thus member of a service much given to writing memoirs; but he was unusual in his knowledge of Europe; with his strong pro-French feelings he was out of tune with Chamberlain's direct methods of negotiation with the dictators, and was removed from effective power in 1938. He wrote *Lessons of My Life* (London, 1943) and left an uncompleted book of memoirs, *The Mist Procession* (London, 1958). He had been private secretary to Baldwin and MacDonald before 1930, and his witty, slightly acid sketches of both men are worth reading. Baldwin 'disguised as an open book', hated roughness and made 'loops' to avoid it. MacDonald came 'in clouds of home-made incense', but he was a good foreign secretary (in 1924) and the 'only member of his Labour Party whose mind approached the first order. It has long been the fashion to deride him, but he played well in his first innings.'[1] Vansittart's papers have been used by Ian Colvin for his *Vansittart in Office* (London, 1965) covering the years 1930–8, using also his own memoranda and reminiscences: Colvin was a newspaper correspondent in Central Europe in the thirties. The steps towards the policy of appeasement are again recounted. Vansittart was early and persistent—perhaps too persistent to be effective—in his warnings against Hitler and Nazi Germany and in his pressure for rearmament. He chafed at the defeatism among the elderly leaders of the time, and ascribed the influence of the Dominions in encouraging this to Lord Lothian's 'kindergarten' contacts. Vansittart, however, made his own mistakes: nominating Sir Nevile Henderson for the German embassy, and framing the

[1] Lord Vansittart, *The Mist Procession* (London, 1958), 323.

Hoare-Laval plan for the partition of Abyssinia. Colvin himself played a part in history: it was his warning to Chamberlain and Halifax, whom he talked to in the House of Commons on 29 March 1938, of an imminent attack on Poland—a false rumour, in fact—that contributed to Chamberlain's change of policy, the offering of guarantees to Poland and other countries against aggression.

No civil servant, but a lone wolf in public life, the writer on military strategy whose voice was more heeded in Germany than in his own country, Captain Sir Basil Liddell Hart knew most of the political leaders from the time of the First World War onwards. His *Memoirs* (2 volumes, London, 1965) are the most important body of reminiscences and experiences published in the sixties. The history of British military and naval policy between the wars—the obsession with the battleship and the cavalry, the rise and fall of the tank, the starts and stops of programmes for mechanising the army, the obscurantism of successive Chiefs of the Imperial General Staff—all is here. There are pictures, not very flattering in some cases, of all the leading generals of 1914–18, especially Haig, Wilson and Robertson (with his 'manner of glum omnipotence'). No one should make any judgment of Lloyd George without reading Liddell Hart, who knew both him and Churchill well, and unhesitatingly puts Lloyd George the first of the two: he and T. E. Lawrence were the two 'most interesting and most gifted' men he knew. The second volume recounts his association with Hore-Belisha at the War Office in 1937–40. The reorganisation of the army and the preparation of the expeditionary force owed much to Liddell Hart's advice; but their relations cooled, Hore-Belisha inevitably ran foul of the generals, and eventually they got him out.

Of Conservatives who wrote their memoirs for these years the most important as a memoirist is L. S. Amery. He was always rather an outsider, a liberal imperialist of the 'kindergarten' type, but never completely of that group, though he was in South Africa as a *Times* correspondent during the Boer War. He was for a time on the staff of the War Cabinet (he was already in

Parliament) and held office in the twenties (a long spell as Colonial Secretary) and as Secretary of State for India in 1940–5; but he was kept out of office in the thirties. Of his three volumes of *My Political Life*, the second and third cover 1914–40 (published in 1953–5). They constitute a detailed personal history of the times, based on a diary he kept, newspapers, published reminiscences and histories, and conversations. The standpoint is always independent. He was opposed to sanctions against Italy over Abyssinia, for example, but was equally an opponent of appeasement and 'Munich', and critical of Baldwin's ineffective leadership. He was one of the dissident Tories of 1938–40 and played his part, as we have seen, in bringing Chamberlain down in 1940. The value of his memoirs is that they record the impressions and later reflections of a well-informed and keen-minded observer.

Robert (later Lord) Boothby published his *I Fight to Live* (London, 1947). He entered Parliament as a young man in 1924, but in spite of his promise and his appointment to minor posts— he was Parliamentary Private Secretary to Churchill in the twenties—he never reached major office. Like Amery he was somewhat of an independent, though hardly an imperialist. He was an admirer of Lloyd George, and an early convert to liberal economic policies of the Keynsian kind, with views akin to those of Harold Macmillan's *Middle Way* (London, 1938). He was at odds with the Conservative leaders from the late twenties, and one of the dissidents opposing Chamberlain in 1938–40. His commentary on the inter-war years is one of the earliest and best.

Three other Conservative memoirists may be picked out. Lord Percy of Newcastle (Lord Eustace Percy) was a protégé of Baldwin's, but his only real office was President of the Board of Education in 1924–9. He is a sympathetic witness to Baldwin's character and personality, and defends him against the charges of indolence and lack of interest in foreign affairs. He denies that there was any split in the Cabinet over the General Strike, or that Baldwin succumbed to any 'wild men' in the midnight breaking off of negotiations with the T.U.C. But he quotes Baldwin as saying to him as they left the meeting, 'Oh, Eustace, I did not sign

on for this.'[1] Lord Eustace's ordinary decency and decent ordinari-
ness make him a useful low-toned witness. Duff Cooper (Lord
Norwich) published *Old Men Forget* in 1953. It is amusing and
readable, and its chief value lies in giving an inside view of
Chamberlain's Cabinet, from which he resigned in protest against
the Munich settlement. It confirms Chamberlain's secretive and
autocratic methods; he consulted his inner circle, Halifax, Simon,
Hoare, and his shadow, Sir Horace Wilson. The Cabinet was
summoned 'to be told what has been done', in the words of the
diary of Sir Alexander Cadogan, Permanent Under-Secretary at
the Foreign Office in 1938.[2] Viscount Swinton (Sir P. Cunliffe-
Lister), who held many offices in the twenties and thirties, and
during the Second World War, was Air Secretary in 1935–8 and
played a large part in the expansion of the R.A.F. Yet Chamberlain dismissed him with little thanks. His *I Remember* (London,
1948) is worth consulting.

Chamberlain, Munich, Baldwin, Abyssinia: these are inevitably
themes in any memoirs of the thirties. One turns with anticipation
to Sir Samuel Hoare's memoirs:[3] here, surely, is the inside story
from one who was certainly of Chamberlain's inner circle, the
'big four' as they were sometimes called. Hoare had a distinguished career, at the Air Ministry, India Office, Home Office,
Admiralty; Baldwin sacrificed him, ending his brief term as
foreign secretary, when public opinion about the Hoare–Laval
proposal over Abyssinia proved hostile, indeed outraged. As one
reads *Nine Troubled Years*, however, one finds only an apologia,
fuller, but no more illuminating to the historian, than the bland
and empty memoirs of Halifax and Simon.[4] Everything was for
the best: Chamberlain's efficiency and vigour were an improvement on Baldwin's leadership, the difference between Chamberlain (and Hoare) and Eden was that the former was inclined to

[1] Lord Percy of Newcastle, *Some Memories* (London, 1938), 135.

[2] Ian Colvin, *Vansittart in Office* (London, 1965), 243.

[3] Lord Templewood (Sir Samuel Hoare), *Nine Troubled Years* (London, 1954).

[4] Lord Simon, *Retrospect* (London, 1952); Lord Halifax, *Fulness of Days*
(London, 1957). Of course, blandness and emptiness can themselves tell the
historian something about all these eminent men.

move step by step to negotiate with the dictators 'until we were militarily stronger', the latter to view policy towards Mussolini and in the Spanish Civil War as a matter of right and wrong. Sir Horace Wilson's role is defended: Chamberlain, like Baldwin, found him invaluable in 'preparing difficult questions for ministerial decision'.[1]

Hoare is persuasive, until one reads his account of Eden's resignation in 1938, in a bare four pages, and contrasts it with Eden's in *Facing the Dictators*, or notices, again from Eden's narrative, that Wilson was far more than the Prime Minister's sounding-board. Eden had other grounds for distrusting Chamberlain: Chamberlain had, in Eden's absence and without consulting him, rebuffed a peace initiative from President Roosevelt (though the extent of the rebuff is arguable); he had also been negotiating with Grandi, the Italian ambassador, independently of Eden. Sir Horace Wilson came to see J. P. L. Thomas, Eden's Parliamentary Private Secretary, and dismissed Roosevelt's initiative as 'woolly rubbish'. Thomas told him that if Eden resigned the American business might leak out and 'the country would then know that the P.M. preferred to turn down the help of a democracy in order that he might pursue his flirtations with the dictators untrammelled. H.W., who was in a towering rage—the first time I have ever seen him in this state—warned me that if America produced the facts he would use the full power of the Government machine in an attack upon A.E.'s past record with regard to the dictators and the shameful obstruction by the F.O. of the P.M.'s attempts to save the peace of the world.'[2]

An interesting question is raised by the memoirs of Labour politicians: why are they so much more numerous than those of the Tories?[3] In a survey made as far back as 1945 at least eighteen

[1] Hoare, *Nine Troubled Years*, 256–7, 260–1.

[2] Eden, *Facing the Dictators*, 563. For the narrative of Roosevelt's proposal, the Chamberlain-Grandi-Eden negotiations and the Cabinet meetings, see 548–97 and appendices, 614–25. For Sir Horace Wilson's interventions, see 447–8, 556, 562–3, 595. See above p. 74.

[3] *Editor*: Can I answer this question? Very many Labour politicians were pro-

Labour memoirs (out of a considerably larger number) were largely concerned with the period 1914–40.[1] Many are of slight importance; some are obviously ghost-written. Some emanate from the turbulent Clydesiders: the best of these are William Gallacher's *Revolt on the Clyde* (London, 1936), on the war-time years, and its sequel, *The Rolling of the Thunder* (London, 1948). To select others is perhaps invidious, but four deserve special mention. Philip (Viscount) Snowden's *Autobiography* was published in two volumes in 1934, after his retirement. It is a lengthy work, covering a career in the Labour movement which began in the heroic days of evangelistic campaigning in the 1890s. More than half is devoted to the years after 1914. It is reminiscence fortified by recourse to newspaper files, and it may be that Snowden's characteristic downrightness makes it seem to ring true. It would, however, be unwise to ignore it for the role of a pacifist Labour member in 1914, for MacDonald's election to the party leadership in 1922, for Labour Cabinet-making in 1924 and 1929 and for the history of the two Labour governments, and above all for the account of the crisis of August 1931, which was written, of course, quite soon after the event. This part, marked by Snowden's animus against MacDonald, though he sided with him in the crisis, has not been superseded (no history of it is complete without quoting MacDonald's remark 'gleefully rubbing his hands: "Yes, to-morrow every Duchess in London will be wanting to kiss me!".')[2] For the history of the first Labour government it should be supplemented by R. W. Lyman's study.[3]

Fenner (Lord) Brockway has written two autobiographical fessional writers, and the naïve self-satisfaction which produces memoirs is a common accompaniment to reforming zeal.

---

[1] C. L. Mowat, 'Some recent books on the British Labour movement', *Journal of Modern History*, XVII, 356–66 (December, 1945); a sequel, 'The history of the Labour Party: the Coles, the Webbs and some others', appeared *ibid.*, XXIII, 146–53 (June, 1951).

[2] P. Snowden, *Autobiography*, Vol. II, 957. R. Bassett's *1931: Political Crisis* (London, 1958), does not, in my view, seriously affect the value of Snowden's narrative.

[3] R. W. Lyman, *The First Labour Government* (London, 1957).

works, *Inside the Left* (London, 1942) and *Outside the Right* (London, 1963). Brockway's political career began in the I.L.P. in 1907; in the war he went to prison as a conscientious objector; he was a leader in the I.L.P. (and briefly an M.P.) in the twenties and thirties; after the disaffiliation of the I.L.P. from the Labour Party in 1932 he remained active in it and in other outlawed left-wing organisations. For the I.L.P., its turbulent relations with Mac-Donald and the two Labour governments, and for the extra-party 'mobilisation of the Left' during and after the Spanish Civil War (Brockway was one of several Labour men who visited the Republican front in Spain) there is no better guide. There are two later studies of Clifford Allen (Lord Allen of Hurtwood), another leader of the I.L.P. until displaced by James Maxton in 1925; he was subsequently one of several amateur 'appeasers'.[1]

Mrs Hamilton (Mary Agnes Hamilton, known as Molly to her friends) was an inveterate writer, from her early novels and works on Greek and Roman history and her several 'campaign biographies' of Ramsay MacDonald, to her life of Arthur Henderson (still the only one there is) and her study of the Webbs. She was a friend of MacDonald until the 1931 crisis, M.P. in 1929–31, and later a governor of the B.B.C. Her memoirs, *Remembering My Good Friends* (London, 1944) has by much the fairest portrait of MacDonald and valuable, sympathetic sketches of Snowden and Allen. She is an important authority for the cross-currents within Labour politics in the twenties (she worked under Ernest Hunter in the I.L.P.'s Information Department, a sort of pro-MacDonald cell within the I.L.P.). Her circle was, however, much wider than the Labour movement, and her reminiscences of Virginia Woolf and Rose Macaulay, F. W. Hirst, the economist, Lord Greene, later Master of the Rolls, and other people eminent in literature and public life are worth reading.

Hugh Dalton, like Eden or Macmillan or Morrison, spans the years from the twenties to the fifties. The first two volumes of his memoirs describe his career to 1945, dividing at 1931. He entered

[1] A. Marwick, *Clifford Allen* (Edinburgh, 1964); M. Gilbert, *Plough My Own Furrow* (London, 1965). See D. C. Watt, *Personalities and Policies*, 124–8.

Parliament in 1924, and was Henderson's under-secretary at the Foreign Office in 1929–31. On Henderson's work, and on the 1931 crisis, he is a useful source. In the thirties he worked hard to win the party away from the negative policy of opposing rearmament while deploring the dictators; he worked also to replace Attlee by Morrison as leader of the Labour Party after the 1935 general election. In the Second World War he was President of the Board of Trade, responsible for economic blockade and 'S.O.E.' (Special Operations Executive). There is no false modesty about Dalton, but his prominence makes his testimony important.[1] Herbert Morrison's two books consist of his *Autobiography* (London, 1960), a chatty book, and *Government and Parliament: a Survey from the Inside* (Oxford, 1954) which is an interesting treatise on the working of the British government by one who had long experience both as an M.P. and as a minister. There is one trade union autobiography of real importance, Walter (Lord) Citrine's *Men and Work* (London, 1964). Citrine, an electrician, became general secretary of the T.U.C. in 1926 and remained so until 1946. He had learned shorthand, and was accustomed to make notes at or immediately after meetings, which made his diary very full; the dialogue which he frequently reproduces is so much the more likely to be authentic. His account of the last-minute negotiations to avert the General Strike (already cited)[2] illustrates the value of his book. It is equally useful for the whole course of the strike, for which he prints his diary, day by day. His pen-portraits of people, the personal touches he introduces in accounts of meetings (with the miners' leaders, for example), are perhaps commonplace, but one is grateful for any detail which calls people to life. It is amusing to compare his long account of a visit to the Webbs at Passfield Corner in 1927 with Mrs Webb's rather supercilious account (which he quotes). Again, he has important information about the meetings of the T.U.C. General Council with MacDonald and Snowden during the August 1931

[1] Hugh Dalton, *Memoirs*, I, *Call Back Yesterday, 1887–1931* (London, 1953); II, *The Fateful Years, 1931–1945* (London, 1957).

[2] See above, p. 72.

crisis—meetings which were important because they were the ground for the charge that the T.U.C. had tried to dictate to the government.

Winston Churchill as writer and subject of memoirs would need a book to himself. For the First World War he wrote *The World Crisis* in five volumes (London, 1923–31): 'Winston has written a book about himself and called it the world crisis' as someone said, not without some justice. This is personal history, seen through the eyes and experiences of a man deeply involved, at the Admiralty, on the Western Front as an officer, as a colleague of Lloyd George in 1917–22. His account of the Anglo-Irish war and of the treaty negotiations in 1921 in which again he was involved, stand out in the final volume entitled *The Aftermath*. For his *Second World War* (London, 1948–54) he wrote six volumes, of which the first, *The Gathering Storm* (London, 1948) traversed the thirties and reached his assumption of the prime ministership. All the volumes are open to criticism, but no more so than anyone's venture into personal history. He is, consciously or not, making a case. He publishes supporting documents. He gives his work the massive weight of his person, his eloquence, his public career beginning in 1900, his unique experience in office in the two wars. *The Gathering Storm* is heavy with his warnings of the ambitions of Hitler and the dangers of delay in rearming; yet there is evidence that he did not become a bitter critic of appeasement until Eden's resignation which, as he says, shook him deeply.[1] Not everyone would accept his judgment of Baldwin in his index: 'confesses to putting party before country.'

One real problem about Churchill in this connection is that (like Beaverbrook, but very much more so) he conceived himself to be writing history but in a fashion produced memoirs. However much he himself appears in the story—and inevitably this is more marked in his treatment of the Second than the First World War—he tried to describe not his part in events but events themselves. Criticism has usually tripped over this difficulty, and the

[1] R. H. Powers, 'Winston Churchill's Parliamentary Commentary on British Foreign Policy, 1935–1938', *Journal of Modern History*, I, 179–82 (June 1954).

failure of the critics shows something about the questions which the historian must ask himself in the face of such material. Critics have fastened on to the fact that Churchill seems much too prominent and all-pervasive in his books. They have attacked his views on higher strategy, his account of particular phases of the fighting, and his omission of parts of the war as experienced by others (especially on the so-called home front). That is to say, they have taken him at his word and have criticised him as an historian. If, however, these massive productions are regarded as memoirs, they fall into place much better. The author's prominence, his defence of particular points of view or schemes, the masses of small personal details, are all appropriate to a book of memoirs and appear as what they are: raw material for historical writing rather than the finished product itself. Thus much of the criticism directed at the works misses its mark. We do not need to enquire whether the wars really were as they looked to Churchill, but we need to know whether the detail he provides is reliable. From such a test the books emerge with great credit. Of course, Churchill is in great part himself to blame for the confusion because he wished to be regarded as the wars' historian; and equally of course, there are ways in which he achieved his ambition. For general reading, *The World Crisis* and *The Second World War* (the former in particular) remain just about the finest single accounts of the towering events they describe. But to the historian they are not history but sources, and as source-material they are memoirs, to be assessed by the usual criteria: was he there, can his description of his activity and thought be corroborated by independent evidence, what exact distortion of the general story is produced by the prism necessarily employed in any approach dominated by personal reminiscence rather than historical method? Any student of contemporary history might be well advised to work his way through one volume of Churchill's with this distinction in mind, for he is likely in that way to learn more about the nature and usefulness of memoirs than pages of instruction can teach him.

Of memoirs which have Churchill as their inspiration the first is Lady Violet Bonham-Carter's *Winston Churchill as I knew him*

(London, 1965): personal, inspired, exciting, sympathetic, showing Churchill as friend and ally of a young woman of brilliant
political gifts, Asquith's daughter who was close in her father's
confidence. The story runs from their first meeting at dinner in
1906 until his loss of office in 1915. Of course any book of reminiscences or biography on any major figure is unlikely to omit
Churchill. For the Second World War one should see him through
American eyes; for instance in Robert E. Sherwood's *White House
Papers of Harry L. Hopkins* (London, 1948), better titled in its
American edition, *Roosevelt and Churchill*. British works of
colleagues or associates of his in the Second World War include
J. W. Wheeler-Bennett (ed.), *Action This Day* (London, 1968) and
G. Pawle, *The War and Colonel Warden* (London, 1963).[1]

Churchill's doctor, Lord Moran, has published *Winston
Churchill: The Struggle for Survival, 1940–1965* (London, 1966). It
is largely extracts from Moran's diary, and it is immensely long. It
has been much criticised; it is a breach of the conduct expected of a
doctor towards his patient; Lord Moran was only on the edge of
Churchill's circle; he misrepresents Churchill's final years as years
of silence and gloom. His critics hit back with revelations of
Moran's requests for office, and of his financial arrangements. The
historian is bound to be grateful to Lord Moran, and it is his task
to test and use the evidence he provides, not to judge whether it
ought to have been given. There is here a treasury of Churchill
stories, his remarks, his dinner-table talk, the course of the great
wartime conferences. There is also the record of his successive
strokes and of the way he remained in office, postponing his
retirement from this date—a Party Conference at which he would
test his recovery—to the next, while his colleagues chafed in
despair. Here, indeed, if not during the later years of the war,
Churchill's physical state may well have influenced the course of
history. But would Eden's succession to the prime ministership in
1952 rather than 1955 have produced more inspiring and pro-
gressive policies for Britain's years of readjustment?

[1] Sub-title of Pawle's book is 'Based on the recollections of Commander
C. R. Thompson . . . Personal Assistant to the Prime Minister 1940–1945'.

Apart from the books by or around Churchill there is little in the way of civilian memoirs about the war and post-war years. Lord Woolton, wartime minister of food, has written his memoirs, but at no great length.[1] The second and third volumes of Harold Macmillan's reminiscences cover the war, for part of which he was minister resident in North Africa, and the post-war years.[2] A former member of the Cabinet Office, Sir George Mallaby, has put down his impressions of three Prime Ministers, Churchill, Attlee and Macmillan, and of some of the generals. He conveys well the atmosphere of a Cabinet meeting under Churchill or Attlee, of the work of secretaries and committees in the War Office, where he was attached to the General Staff, and of the big wartime conferences at Cairo and Quebec.[3] The second volume of Eden's memoirs (*The Reckoning*, 1965) covers the war years, the third (*Full Circle*, 1960) the postwar, culminating in Suez. As always, Eden concentrates on foreign policy, is full, quotes extensively from letters and speeches, but seldom breaks the barrier of suave discretion.

Nor are the Labour governments of 1945–51 and the Conservative governments after 1951 much better served. Attlee's reminiscences, *As It Happened* (London, 1954), are as flat as the title and as laconic as the man. Here is an example. In 1927, Attlee and the other members of the Simon Commission visited India. To this visit he devotes two brief paragraphs, including these two sentences:

> No untoward incident occurred though a bomb had been prepared for us. Its custodian, however, dropped it from the rack of a railway carriage with unfortunate results for himself.[4]

After this it is no surprise that he devotes no more than seven pages to the wartime government, in which he was deputy Prime

[1] Lord Woolton, *Memoirs* (London, 1959).
[2] Harold Macmillan, *The Blast of War* (London, 1967); *Tides of Fortune* (London, 1969).
[3] Sir George Mallaby, *From My Level: Unwritten Minutes* (London, 1965).
[4] C. R. Attlee, *As it Happened* (London, 1954), 64.

Minister. The Labour governments get five short chapters. This might have been made good by Francis Williams' *A Prime Minister Remembers* (London, 1961), which is based on tape-recorded conversations with Attlee and is presented partly in dialogue form. We are not much the wiser. There is some discussion of the plan to displace him as leader of the party, and therefore as Prime Minister, in 1945 when Churchill resigned; Morrison was again being run for the office. The book does contain several letters reproduced *in extenso*, including three to President Truman over the development of the peaceful uses of atomic energy and the making of a British atom bomb. This followed the renewed non-co-operation between the United States and Britain in this field when Congress passed the Mc-Mahon bill. For a decision on policy of fundamental importance even this account, loquacious in comparison beside the two pages given to the subject (mostly taken up with Attlee's visit to Washington in this connection in November 1945) in *As it Happened*, is singularly uninformative.

There is more life in Dalton's third volume of memoirs, *High Tide and After* (London, 1962), in which the post-war Labour governments have pride of place: the *annus mirabilis* of 1946, when Dalton went about 'with a song in my heart' and Hartley Shaw-cross proclaimed 'we are masters now', and the *annus horrendus* of 1947.

As for the thirteen years of Conservative rule under Churchill, Eden, Macmillan and Douglas-Home after 1951, the cupboard of memoirs is almost bare. Lord Kilmuir (Sir David Maxwell Fyfe) has published his memoirs, *Political Adventure* (London, 1964). He entered Parliament in 1935 when he was already a K.C. He was Home Secretary and later Lord Chancellor in the fifties, until he was dismissed in Macmillan's purge of 13 July 1962. He is un-apologetic about Suez, and reveals nothing more than the Cabinet's timetable of meetings at the time. He does, however, give vent to the shrill bitterness which most Conservatives then felt towards the Labour Opposition, and especially towards Hugh Gaitskell. Earlier, he gives useful sketches of some of his colleagues in the Cabinet in 1951. However, there is one slim book of reminiscence and exhortation which deserves to become the *locus classicus* for a brief description of the Conservative Party, Macmillan and its other leaders, and the continuing power of the 'Establishment' in the fifties, Reginald Bevins' *The Greasy Pole* (London, 1965). Bevins, a working man from Liverpool, was Parliamentary Private Secretary to Macmillan at the Ministry of Housing, and after holding minor offices was Postmaster General until the defeat of the Conservatives in 1964, when he lost his seat. He is scornful about his colleagues' efforts to soften his opposition in 1963 to the agreed plan, which he stuck to and won, to charge higher rentals to the commercial television companies. He has no great respect for the civil service. When asked by the Chief Whip in 1963 whom he favoured as Macmillan's successor, 'What about the peers—Alec and the other one', he replied instantly, 'Not at any bloody price.'[1] Would that more writers of memoirs had his candour!

There is another large class of memoirs which historians are likely to neglect, literary and personal. Perhaps they are right: the glimpses they give of everyday life and changing customs and ideas in society, whether high or low, may not repay the time spent, however enjoyably, in reading them. But a good deal of readily forgotten social history may be extracted from such books, especially in an age of rapid social change. Here we are on the borders between fact and fiction; a writer's autobiography is bound to be a work of art, emotion remembered in tranquillity, the colours of childhood so much brighter than they ever were on sea or land. Even the memoirs of ordinary people can never be just that. Ordinary people are inarticulate, or at least they never write anything more than a letter or a report; to put one's life before the public between the covers of a book argues some force or ambition out of the ordinary. There are autobiographies of working men and women, and it would be useful if one could supply an annotated list. There are autobiographies of country people, successors to Laura Thompson's *Larkrise to Candleford*, an

[1] R. Bevins, *The Greasy Pole* (London, 1965), 143.

evocation of a Victorian childhood in a remote Oxfordshire hamlet; examples are Fred Kitchen's *Brother to the Ox* (London, 1940) or Laurie Lee's *Cider with Rosie* (London, 1959) or Arthur Randell's *Sixty Years a Fenman* (London, 1966) and *Fenland Railwaymen* (London, 1968). Ray Gosling's *Sum Total* (London, 1962) recaptures youth in the provinces after the Second World War; Richard Hoggart's *Uses of Literacy* (London, 1957) breathes nostalgia for a working-class childhood in Leeds. The First World War produced scores of books of survivors from the trenches; a rare one by a private is Frank Richards' *Old Soldiers Never Die* (London, 1933). Other examples of what ordinary people can write, recalling the thirties quite as vividly as a novel like William Cooper's *Scenes from Provincial Life*, are Hubert Nicholson, *Half My Days and Nights* (London, 1941) and Nerina Shute, *We Mixed Our Drinks* (London, 1945). On another level one can learn much of the 'below stairs' history of the B.B.C. from former members of its staff; R. S. Lambert's *Ariel and All His Quality: An Impression of the B.B.C. from Within* (London, 1940) and Maurice Gorham, *Sound and Fury: 21 Years in the B.B.C.* (London, 1948) are examples. For the gay life of the young in high society in the twenties, one should read Daphne Fielding's *Mercury Presides* (London, 1954), a real-life version of Waugh's *Vile Bodies*. Daphne, daughter of Lord Vivian, married the heir of the Marquess of Bath.

The wealth of literary memoirs makes selection essential. Sir Osbert Sitwell's *Laughter in the Next Room* (Boston, 1948), the fourth volume of his autobiography, encompassed the war of 1914–18 and the post-war years, and the eccentricities of his father, Sir George, and his sister. This was another part of the forest of literary and artistic life. The best of the literary autobiographies of this century is David Garnett's *Golden Echo* (London, 1953)—youth in Edwardian England—followed by *The Flowers of the Forest* (London, 1955) and *The Familiar Faces* (London, 1962). Garnett joined the Bloomsbury circle, and his memories of parties, charades and play-readings in 1915 and of Garsington Manor, where Lady Ottoline Morrell gave refuge to a number of conscientious objectors during the war, are gay and amusing; later he and Duncan Grant worked as farm labourers in Suffolk and Sussex, performing non-combatant national service. The third volume, which ends in 1940, mixes the private and literary worlds with the political: Spain and Munich provide the menacing undertones.[1]

An autobiography of wider scope, which has been called 'the outstanding autobiography of our time',[2] is that of Leonard Woolf. Of the five volumes published, the third and fourth, *Beginning Again* (London, 1964) and *Downhill All the Way* (London, 1967) are devoted to the years between 1911, when Woolf left the Colonial service in Ceylon (he married Virginia Stephen in 1912) and 1939. *Beginning Again* describes country life in Rodmell, near Lewes, the founding of the Hogarth Press, life in Bloomsbury, a visit to Garsington, memories of Katherine Mansfield and Middleton Murry, and above all the first of Virginia Woolf's breakdowns, which lasted from 1913 to 1915: Woolf's devotion then and later saved her life and made possible the writing of her novels. This may be dismissed as literary history or fireside reading—and so it is, of the kind that gives deep pleasure. Woolf, however, was for many years one of the intellectual leaders in the Labour Party, presiding over committees on questions of foreign and colonial policy—about the latter he wrote important books. He was at the socialists' Leeds Convention of 3 June 1917; he knew the Webbs, Bob Smillie, the miners' leader, and Ernest Bevin, and also Ramsay MacDonald, of whom he writes, 'I have never known a vainer and more treacherous man than Ramsay . . . one of his most marked characteristics was tortuousness of mind',[3] of which he gives several examples. The fourth volume continues the same themes; a visit to Germany in May 1935 gave premonitions of the wrath to come.

A few words about Ireland; for no account of the value of

---

[1] I have described Garnett's memoirs and several others in 'From the Edwardian Age to the Thirties: some literary memoirs', *Critical Quarterly*, V, 157–67 (Summer 1963).

[2] W. A. Robson in *New Statesman*, 22 August 1969.

[3] L. Woolf, *Beginning Again* (London, 1964), 219, 221.

memoirs for recent *British* history would be complete without
reference to the extraordinary richness of this source for the
history of the Easter Rising of 1916 and the Anglo-Irish war of
1919–21. It is true that there is a great lack of memoirs from the
Unionist or English side: General Sir Nevil Macready's *Annals
of an Active Life* (two volumes, London, 1924) and the memoirs of
the eccentric Brigadier F. P. Crozier, a Unionist officer who was
in command of the Auxiliary Division of the Royal Irish Constabulary in 1920 and resigned in disgust over Black and Tan
atrocities, are the only works that come to mind.[1] Hugh Martin,
at the time a reporter for the *Daily News*, wrote of his experiences,
which included threats of violence by the Black and Tans for his
frank reports of their behaviour in Tralee in November 1920; he
was typical of English newspaper correspondents whose reports
helped to turn the British public against the war being fought in
their name.[2] Irish memoirs of the Black and Tan war include
those of Darrell Figgis, Charles Dalton, Ernie O'Malley, Desmond
Ryan, Dan Breen, Frank Gallagher and Patrick McCartan.[3] Here
is captured some of the flavour and fury of life in Dublin under
military occupation and of the ambushes and raids of the I.R.A.
brigades in the country. The very obvious *parti pris* needs no
stressing and—just because for once it is so obvious—forms no
problem for the historian.[4]

[1] F. P. Crozier, *Ireland for Ever* (London, 1932) and *Impressions and Recollections* (London, 1930).

[2] Hugh Martin, *Ireland in Insurrection* (London, 1921).

[3] Darrell Figgis, *Recollections of the Irish War* (London, 1927); Charles Dalton,
With the Dublin Brigade (London, 1929); E. O'Malley, *Army without Banners*
(London, 1936, English title, *On Another Man's Wound*; paperback edition,
1961); D. Ryan, *Remembering Sion* (London, 1934); Dan Breen, *My Fight for
Irish Freedom* (Dublin, 1924; paperback edition, 1964); Frank Gallagher (pseud.
D. Hogan), *Four Glorious Years* (Dublin, 1953); P. McCartan, *With de Valera in
America* (London, 1932).

[4] See my use of such material in *Britain between the Wars*, 57–72. There has
been no full-scale scholarly history of the Black and Tan war, making critical
use of the wealth of memoirs and other materials in existence. No doubt this
deficiency will soon be filled by Irish historians. The Irish government has been
gathering material in its Bureau of Military History, but so far this has been
kept under lock and key.

For the Easter Rising there was an early personal account of day-to-day life in Dublin by a non-participant, the writer James Stephens, *Insurrection in Dublin* (Dublin, 1916; paperback 1966). The fiftieth anniversary of the Rising brought some further reminiscences as well as a paperback explosion (in Dublin) of popular histories of the heroes and episodes of the Rising and of the Black and Tan war. The reminiscences include Sean Mac-Entee's *Episode at Easter* (Dublin, 1966), interesting because the author lived at Dundalk and took part in the affray at Castlebellingham—one of the very few incidents which occurred outside Dublin—in which a policeman was killed; subsequently he made his way to Dublin by cart and on foot in time to take part in the Rising in the city. M. J. O'Connor's *Stone Walls . . .* (1966), another paperback, is valuable as a rare record of the prison life in Wales which many of the participants experienced. Bulmer Hobson, another prominent but long-silent survivor, published his *Ireland Yesterday and Tomorrow* in 1968 and his 'Foundation and growth of the Irish Volunteers, 1913–14' in 1963.[1] Desmond Fitzgerald's *Memoirs 1913–1916* appeared posthumously in 1968.

The volume of material now available on the Rising (not all of it by any means consists of memoirs) is witnessed to by two articles by F. X. Martin. These constitute a lengthy and dispassionate critical review of much controversial and contradictory evidence. It is a pity that such necessary tasks of criticism have so rarely been undertaken for other parts of recent British history.[2]

All the material reviewed in this chapter is marked by the personal involvement in the affairs described of the man who produced it. All of it is therefore exceptionally important and exceptionally difficult. Material of this kind is unusually plentiful for the period here treated and to some extent compensates for the relative dearth of more official, less personal, more objective

[1] In F. X. Martin, ed., *The Irish Volunteers, 1913–1915: Recollections and Documents* (Dublin, 1963).
[2] F. X. Martin, '1916—Myth, Fact and Mystery', *Studia Hibernica*, No. 7 (1968), 7–124; 'The 1916 Rising—a *Coup d'État* or a "Bloody Protest"?', *ibid.*, No. 8 (1968), 106–37.

material. But since the personal type of material can be effectively criticised only by means of the impersonal, the historian is bound to walk frequently a treacherous ground. Until more is known against which these memoirs and diaries can be checked, the only advice one can give him is to read very widely and judge very cautiously. Especially he must forever remain aware that any historical reconstruction in which this type of material plays so large a part is provisional and not likely to be very reliable. More than any others of our sources, memoirs and their like bring home the problems of contemporary history.

CHAPTER 5

Contemporary Writing

Anything written at the time, that is to say contemporaneously, or nearly so, with events or situations which the historian will later describe or analyse or categorise, is a potential source. We accept and act upon this without question when the document is a letter or paper in the government's records or in a collection of family manuscripts. We accept this equally with newspapers and other periodicals. We may not, perhaps, be so ready to accord the status to a book on current affairs—politics or economics or sociology, for example. Yet it is obvious that almost any discussion of institutions—such as W. Ivor Jennings' standard works on *Parliament* (Cambridge, 1940) and *Cabinet Government* (Cambridge, 1936)—will be partly historical, partly descriptive of the situation as it is, a description which itself becomes in time historical. This is even more obvious in the case of a particular kind of study in which the twentieth century has been prolific—though its ancestry is very much older—the social survey.

There may be difficulty in finding out what books of this sort exist for a period forty or fifty years back—or, for that matter, much further back. Some will eventually find their way into historical bibliographies. Some can be traced in the subject entries in *Whitaker's Cumulative Book List* or the *British National Bibliography*. The *British Museum Subject Index*, published at intervals, is useful, and also the *Subject Index of the London Library*, of which editions appeared in 1923, 1938 and 1955. The *London Bibliography of the Social Sciences* was published by the London School of Economics in four volumes in 1932, and has been kept nearly up-to-date with several supplements.

Contemporary books which can serve as sources must be distinguished from contemporary books which are not sources but pieces of history in themselves. One would not go to J. M.

Keynes' *Economic Consequences of the Peace* (London, 1919) to find information about the peace treaties and reparations (though historians have borrowed Keynes' amusing and malicious sketches of Wilson and Clemenceau from it); its publication was a historical event, starting the revulsion from the Versailles settlement with which the British public was haunted for the next twenty years. R. H. Tawney's *Acquisitive Society* (London, 1921) was another tract for the times, describing a utopia in which service and function, not property, determined a man's place and livelihood. John Strachey's *Coming Struggle for Power* (London, 1932), foreshadowing the triumph of communism, is a historical fact but not a source. So are pseudonymous works such as 'Cato', *Guilty Men* (London, 1940), though they may be useful repositories of gossip.

I. CURRENT AFFAIRS

Since any book on current affairs may prove to be a source, and the category is a very large one, it may be useful to group some examples into several types. A large group is that of descriptive works. G. D. H. Cole's *Organised Labour* (London, 1924) is an example of many books describing and sometimes criticising the trade unions down the years. Vera Brittain's *Women's Work in Modern England* (London, 1928) or A. M. Carr-Saunders and P. A. Wilson, *The Professions* (Oxford, 1933), W. H. Wickwar, *The Public Services* (London, 1938) and H. H. Ballin, *Organization of Electricity Supply in Great Britain* (London, 1946) are other examples of this class. Books on unemployment policies (R. C. Davison, *The Unemployed: old policies and new*, London, 1929), on education (J. Dover Wilson, ed., *Schools of England*, London, 1928), social services (M. Penelope Hall, *Social Services in Modern England*, London, 1952), housing estates (T. Young, *Becontree and Dagenham*, London, 1934), films (Paul Rotha, *The Film till now*, London, 1930) are both descriptive and historical. C. F. G. Masterman's *England after War* (London, 1923) is an example of a deliberate attempt to survey one's own time and condition; Laurence

Thompson's *Portrait of England* (London, 1952) is another representative of this large class of books. So, in a different way, is the last part of Raymond Williams' *Long Revolution* (London, 1961), in which he carries his criticism of culture and society into the 1950s. Such books can be of great help to the historian, provided he takes account of the writer's opportunities for observation and of his standpoint, foibles and limitations—in fact, subjects his evidence to the usual critical tests. G. D. H. Cole compiled two such charts of the statistics of the times, *Condition of Britain* (London, 1937) with Margaret Cole, and *Post-war Condition of Britain* (London, 1956), in which chapters on class, income, poverty, housing, education and much more are fully illustrated by tables. D. V. Glass' *British Social Mobility* (London, 1954) is one of the few British works of its kind, examining changes in the class structure, and the degree to which social mobility has increased, on the basis of investigations in 1949–52.

Other useful books have been written as tracts to advocate or criticise some aspect of public policy, but in so doing they give information which is either historical or quickly becomes so. Thus, J. F. S. Ross' *Parliamentary Representation* (London, 1943) attacks misrepresentation, but in doing so provides useful statistics about the parliaments elected since 1918. Kenneth Lindsay's *Social Progress and Educational Waste* (London, 1926) was a tract against the inequality of opportunity for secondary education which existed for children in different districts or cities, and it argued that 'proved ability' in at least forty per cent of the nation's children was being denied expression. To prove its points it had to provide historical information about the number of secondary school places in different areas. Books on the farm problem of the twenties, or the unused potentialities of hill lands, have long since become historical sources.[1] A book on drinking in the First World War and the government's measures for its control, including the

[1] E. J. Russell, *The Farm and the Nation* (London, 1933); Viscount Astor and B. Seebohm Rowntree, *British Agriculture: the Principles of Future Policy* (London, 1938); R. G. Stapledon, *Hill Lands of Britain: development or decay?* (London, 1937).

state ownership of public houses in Carlisle and Gretna, is a mixture of exhortation and history.[1]

Another type of contemporary work is more consciously historical. Caroline Playne, an early psychologist, wrote two books on the reaction of the civilian population to the war which are near enough to the time to be prime sources for social history, *Society at War, 1914–1916* (London, 1931) and *Britain Holds On, 1917–1918* (London, 1936). A man calling himself 'I.O.' (Irish Officer?) wrote a valuable account of the Black and Tan war in Ireland (*Administration of Ireland, 1920* [London, 1921]), and followed this by a book under his own name, C. J. C. Street, *Ireland in 1921* (London, 1922). The well-known series of books on British general elections, beginning with R. B. McCallum and Alison Readman, *The British General Election of 1945* (London, 1947) provides many examples of this *genre*. Mark Abrams' *Condition of the British People, 1911–1945* (London, 1945), the work of a distinguished social statistician and advertising man, belongs in the same class.

Journalists are, of course, contemporary historians, whether consciously or not. A book written within months or at most a year of the events it describes is certainly contemporary, and even if its judgments do not stand the test of time it remains an important source of contemporary attitudes and impressions. The approach of war in the late thirties produced many such works of journalists: G. E. R. Gedye's *Fallen Bastions: the Central European Tragedy* (London, 1939), and Douglas Reed's *Insanity Fair* (London, 1938) and *Disgrace Abounding* (London, 1939) are representative. The passions roused by the Spanish Civil War stimulated much writing; the Duchess of Atholl's Penguin book, *Searchlight on Spain* (London, 1938) is an excellent example. An early exploration of post-war Europe and the Cold War is Chester Wilmot's *Struggle for Europe* (London, 1952). Similarly, for the Blitz and the war on the home front from 1940 to 1945 the historian must turn to the contemporary works of journalists and other observers, and to accounts, partly autobiographical, written

[1] A. Shadwell, *Drink in 1914–22: a Lesson in Control* (London, 1923).

soon afterwards. The wealth to be found in such sources is indicated in the bibliographical section on the Blitz in Angus Calder's *The People's War* (London, 1969), 629–30.

The depression of the 1930s produced many books of this kind, documentaries which shade into history. Several were published by the Left Book Club, but if 'facts are sacred' this makes no difference to their historical content, while their views are in themselves part of history. George Orwell's *Road to Wigan Pier*, Ellen Wilkinson's *Town that was Murdered* [Jarrow], G. C. M. M'Gonigle and J. Kirby's *Poverty and Public Health* (London, 1936), the Pilgrim Trust's *Men without Work* (London, 1938) and J. B. Priestley's *English Journey* (London, 1934), Hilda Jennings' *Brynmawr* (London, 1934) and even John Boyd Orr's *Food Health and Income* (London, 1936) are prime sources (one's doubts about the last-named turn on the point that Orr's figures of malnutrition were based on a very small sample survey and may have exaggerated the degree of suffering; but the book became an argument for more intervention by the government in the cause of the nation's health, and so itself entered into history).

The line between reporting and advocacy is necessarily thin. In 1931 P.E.P. (Political and Economic Planning) was founded as a private organisation to study and report on industrial problems. It issued in the next four years a notable series of reports on the location of industry, the health and social services, the press, agriculture and other matters, each a mine of historical information on its subject. The same applies to the works of economists. The Economic Science and Statistics section of the British Association for the Advancement of Science published two valuable collaborative works, *Britain in Depression* (1935) and *Britain in Recovery* (1938). Ernest Davies' *'National' Capitalism: the Government's Record as Protector of Private Monopoly* (London, 1939) can be balanced against A. F. Lucas, *Industrial Reconstruction and the Control of Competition* (London, 1937). Economists were perhaps especially prolific in semi-historical current affairs studies during the depressed thirties, and there is no need to prolong the list save to mention the works of A. L. Bowley and Colin Clark on national income and the standard of living.[1] More recent examples include William Davis' *Three Years Hard Labour* (London, 1968). Similarly, the works of sociologists soon have a historical use, either because of the facts they record or from the point of view which they represent. An example is R. M. Titmuss, *Income Distribution and Social Change* (London, 1962), which demonstrates the persistence of private wealth within the welfare state.

2. SOCIAL SURVEYS

The social survey may seem a fairly new tool of the sociologist, going back no further than Charles Booth's *Life and Labour of the People of London* of the 1890s. Of course it is much older, even if it was not quite as 'sophisticated' as it is today. The oldest national survey in England was Domesday Book; the most continuous one since 1801 has been the Census. For Scotland Sir John Sinclair of the Board of Agriculture instituted the *Statistical Account of Scotland* in the 1790s; it has had two successors. Sir F. M. Eden's *State of the Poor* (1797) was a forerunner of several early nineteenth-century investigations. Booth's survey was followed by others, of which the most famous is B. Seebohm Rowntree's *Poverty* (London, 1901), a study of York in 1899 based not upon a sample of households (as in later surveys) but on visits to every house in the city. A study of Norwich, and another of four towns, Warrington, Northampton, Bolton and Stanley (County Durham) in 1910–11, followed before the war.[2]

What can social surveys provide for the historian?[3] For the twenties there were very few, though Professor Bowley re-surveyed the towns examined in 1910–11 and found that the proportion of working-class families in poverty was little more

[1] A. L. Bowley, *Studies in National Income, 1924–1938* (Cambridge, 1942); C. Clark, *National Income and Outlay* (London, 1937) and *Conditions of Economic Progress* (London, 1940, 1951).

[2] C. B. Hawkins, *Norwich: A Social Study* (London, 1910); A. L. Bowley and A. R. Burnett-Hurst, *Livelihood and Poverty* (London, 1915).

[3] There are useful accounts of the methods and limitations of surveys by D. Caradog Jones, *Social Surveys* (London, 1949) and Mark Abrams, *Social Surveys and Social Action* (London, 1951).

than half that of the earlier survey.[1] Poverty and its extent was, indeed, a main subject for investigation in the early social surveys, but the scope has widened to include the way of life of households of different classes, institutions, habits, uses of leisure; and indeed many of Charles Booth's volumes were devoted to religious organisation in London. Perhaps the work of the two American sociologists, R. S. and Helen M. Lynd's *Middletown* (London, 1929), a study of Muncie, Indiana, contributed to this change, though there has been no British 'Middletown'. Indeed, in the depression of the thirties poverty, unemployment and poor housing were inevitably the focus of the social surveys which then blossomed forth.

The three volumes of the *Social Survey of Merseyside*, edited by D. Caradog Jones of the University of Liverpool Social Science Department and published in 1934, may serve as representative. It was based on a random sample of every thirtieth house, taken from the Voter's Register and, as with Booth's survey, the investigators were school attendance officers. The first volume was partly historical and considered the growth of population, native and immigrant, housing, rent, income, poverty, and working-class family budgets. Volume two surveyed industries, occupations, mobility, earnings, employment, and examined the port, transport, distribution, building, manufacturing, domestic and clerical employment, and unemployment generally. Volume three dealt with local government, public health, education, adolescents, broken families, pensioners, leisure, religion, the social services, future population trends and, unusually, with several 'sub-normal types' including the blind and deaf, the mentally deficient, alcoholics, criminals and the sick. From this survey it is possible (to give one example only) to discover the actual decline in the number of households with domestic servants between 1911 and 1921 (in Liverpool from 13·5 to 8·3 per 100 families; in Wallasey from 22·4 to 14·5).

Among students of society B. Seebohm Rowntree was unique in that a long life and a persistent curiosity enabled him to re-

[1] A. L. Bowley and M. M. Hogg, *Has Poverty Diminished?* (London, 1925).

survey York in 1936, a generation after his pioneer survey of 1899. In 1899 he had found 15·5 per cent of the working class in poverty (and as many more on the poverty line); in 1936 on the same standard the proportion was 6·8 per cent (*Poverty and Progress* [London, 1941]). However, applying a slightly more generous 'human needs' standard he now found 14·2 per cent of the working population in abject poverty and 31·1 per cent below the poverty line. In a last and much briefer survey, in 1950, he found that the 'welfare state' had virtually eliminated the former poverty.[1] His interest had by then turned to the uses people made of their leisure.[2] Other surveys of the thirties include P. Ford, *Work and Wealth at a Modern Port* (London, 1934), a study of Southampton, and Herbert Tout's brief but admirable *Standard of Living in Bristol* (Bristol, 1938), in which 10·7 per cent of Bristol working-class families were shown to be below the poverty line. London was re-surveyed in nine volumes, the *New Survey of London Life and Labour* (London, 1930–5), edited by Sir H. Llewellyn Smith.

Other surveys connected with town and country planning, and industrial surveys, have much to offer the historian, though they must be distinguished from social surveys. C. S. Orwin's *Country Planning* (Oxford, 1944), a study of the Banbury area, and the *Second Industrial Survey of South Wales* (Cardiff, 1937)[3] are representative. F. Fraser Darling's *West Highland Survey* (Oxford, 1955) takes us into the field of human ecology. Plans for reconstruction after the Second World War gave rise to many town planning studies.[4] Since the war there have been sociological studies of

[1] B. S. Rowntree and G. R. Lavers, *Poverty and the Welfare State* (London, 1951).
[2] *English Life and Leisure* (London, 1951).
[3] Edited by H. A. Marquand in the University College of South Wales: 3 volumes.
[4] West Midland Group, *Conurbation* (London, 1948), a study of Birmingham; *Social Aspects of a Town Development Plan* (Liverpool, 1951), a study of Dudley by the Liverpool University Department of Social Science; J. Glaisyer *et al.*, *County Town: a Civic Survey for the Planning of Worcester* (London, 1946); *English Country: a planning survey of Herefordshire* (London, 1946); Sir P. Abercrombie, *The Greater London Plan* (London, 1945).

English and Welsh villages,[1] of country towns,[2] larger towns,[3] and a new town.[4] There has also been a very interesting study of the contrasting ways of life of families in Bethnal Green and their kinsfolk uprooted and moved out to Debden.[5] No doubt future historians will find grist in all these works.

A variant of this sort of material are the reports of Mass-Observation. This organisation was started in 1937 by John Madge and Tom Harrison and published its first report, *Britain by Mass-Observation*, in 1939, much of it devoted to attitudes over the Munich settlement. Its files have been used to good effect in Angus Calder's *The People's War* (London, 1969). Among its later studies was one on the Coronation in 1953, *May 12th.* Mass-Observation used five different methods of discovering public attitudes: direct interviewing, probing in the course of casual, 'free' conversations, noting of remarks overheard, direct observation, and autobiographical, statements, diaries and letters.[6]

Mass-Observation, public opinion polls and market research have obvious affinities. Recent work by Mass-Observation Limited (the suffix is significant) has been in these latter areas.[7] Public opinion polls were first developed in the United States in connection with presidential elections; the *Literary Digest* was a pioneer, followed by the more scientific polls of George Gallup and Elmo Roper. In Britain the idea was taken up rather slowly. There is the British Institute of Public Opinion, and in 1948 the

[1] W. M. Williams, *Sociology of an English Village: Gosforth* (London, 1956); D. Jenkins *et al.*, *Welsh Rural Communities* (Cardiff, 1960).

[2] Margaret Stacey, *Tradition and Change: a study of Banbury* (Oxford, 1960).

[3] T. Cauter and J. S. Downham, *The Communication of Ideas* (London, 1954) —Derby. See also T. Brennan *et al.*, *Social Change in South-West Wales* (London, 1954).

[4] H. Orlans, *Stevenage: A Sociological Study of a New Town* (London, 1953).

[5] M. Young and P. Willmott, *Family Kinship in East London* (London, 1957).

[6] For criticism of Mass-Observation's methods see M. Abrams, *Social Surveys and Social Action*, 105–13.

[7] Ralph Harris and A. Seldon, *Choice in Welfare: Second report of an enquiry conducted by Mass-Observation Limited into the extent of knowledge and preference in state and private provision for education, health services and pensions* (London, 1965).

weekly, *Picture Post*, began making quarterly surveys of political opinion, followed later by various newspapers. Mark Abrams describes as 'borrowers' from social surveys both the public opinion polls and the whole business of market research. Market research might seem to be alien to the historian, but the Hulton Readership Survey published a book, *Patterns of British Life*, in 1950, which shows its value for him. It divided the population into five income groups, well-to-do, middle class, lower middle class, working class and 'poor', and assessed the improvement in wages, salaries and standard of living since 1914 and 1939. On a popular but none the less important level, an advertising man has written a book on the marked diversities in tastes, food, clothing and living habits generally in the different parts of Great Britain; this is based on information from hundreds of marketing and other surveys, reported both in the general press and in specialised periodicals such as *Retail Business* and the *Advertiser's Weekly*.[1]

The fundamental problems of this type of material, both obvious, are two. How accurate and full was the collection of data, and how accurate and free of preconceived notions was the working out of the data? The notorious failure of the public opinion polls in the 1970 election underlined both points. Of course, the techniques have been increasingly refined, or at least standardised, and the widespread scepticism once prevalent may not be so justified now. There certainly can be no universally valid answer to the questions they raise for the historian, but certain guide-lines can be offered. First, there is a distinction between a purely quantitative survey (like a census) and those in which quantitative elements are admitted (Mass-Observation most obviously, but also every social survey yet made). The first is likely to be more reliable but markedly less informative because it confines itself to questions which can be reduced to pure statistics. The reliability of the second depends on the elements which every practitioner of the method has drilled into him. The historian similarly should be aware of these elements, which include the

[1] D. Elliston Allen, *British Tastes: An enquiry into the likes and dislikes of the Regional Consumer* (London, 1968); see his instructive footnotes.

form of the question put, the size and nature of the sample, the training of the enquirers used, and the manner in which the results are presented in tables (or graphs) and in continuous prose. When using such a survey, the historian needs first to be quite clear about the questions which it attempted to answer; it is not likely that he will benefit from the result if he tacitly substitutes a question of his own, but this happens. Moreover, he needs to consider the precise form of the question put which can be so phrased as to condition the result. He should make certain that the area from which the information is obtained is fairly and properly designated, and any survey which does not enable him to check this is probably best discarded. He needs to consider more carefully than the surveyors do that people can give deliberately misleading answers. And in considering the result, he should be on the alert not only for plain error (unintentional or deliberate), but, more important, for the intrusion of emotive or loaded terms, value judgements parading as reported fact, variations of emphasis. In short, he needs to do at least some critical appraising and check-ing of even the most finished-looking survey before he can use it. If he finds it short of perfection, he can still use it, but less simply. In practice, historians, untrained in both survey techniques and statistics, are only too likely either to swallow all that is put before them or to allow their own prejudices to do duty for critical assessment: they believe results that suit them and discard those that cut across their preferences. Such methods are unfair to the historian and the survey-maker alike.

3. NOVELS, POETRY, PLAYS

'Without appreciating good literature no one will really under-stand the nature of society.'[1] Historians of all periods pay lip-service to the idea that a thorough knowledge of the literature of the time is essential to an understanding of its history; much fewer

---

[1] Richard Hoggart, 'Literature and Society', in *A Guide to the Social Sciences*, ed. Andrew MacKenzie (London, 1966), 225—an excellent introduction to the subject.

possess and apply this knowledge. What they are more likely to do is to use literature as a quarry for 'background' material: a snatch of dialogue, a description of a ceremony, a scene from the streets or the drawing room. This, as Richard Hoggart has argued, is 'working *from outside literature* . . . rather than allowing literature to provide in its own right a form of new and distinctive knowledge about society'. The illustrative value of a work of literature depends on its intrinsic power: 'properly read—read in and for themselves, with an openness to the author's imagination and art —works of literature give an insight into the life of an age, a kind and intensity of insight, which no other source can give'.[1] Literature can reveal the meaning of things, a point which Hoggart illustrates from chapter 74 of George Eliot's *Middlemarch*, in which Mrs Bulstrode, the banker's wife, discovers the secret of her husband's past and comes to accept the change in her station in Middlemarch society.

The trouble is that any reference to novels, to take the most obvious branch of literature for historians to use, is bound to be highly personal, depending on what one has read or remembered, and even more on what one has not read. And having made his choice the historian can usually say no more than that it reflects the spirit of the time—and then perhaps use it for a little quarrying. Richard Aldington's *Death of a Hero* thus stands for a number of novels about the war of 1914–8, the hero's thoughts and actions, as a civilian, a youth, a soldier thrust into the horrors of trench warfare, supplementing impressions from the host of war memoirs. By contrast, H. G. Wells' *Mr Britling Sees It Through* seems much more of a chronicle of the home front in fictional form, without the sense of wholeness for which Hoggart looks. D. H. Lawrence, though he wrote much in the twenties, does not really say much of general application. *Women in Love* describes the harsh industrial scene in the Nottinghamshire coalfield, and caricatures Lady Ottoline Morrell and her set—better seen from the memoirs of David Garnett or Bertrand Russell. *Kangaroo*, though set in Australia, has a long digression on Lawrence's

[1] *Ibid.*, 225–6.

loathing of the war mentality and his disgust at being examined for military service; it also conveys the feelings of comradeship and a narrow patriotism on the part of the ex-servicemen, though in Australia rather than Britain.

For the twenties the historian is likely to turn to the novels of Aldous Huxley or Evelyn Waugh. But how representative are they? They are set among a small part of the upper middle class—a part of London and Oxford, a part of England. Of course no novel can give insight into the whole of society. *Point Counter-Point* or *Antic Hay* conveys the sort of feeling of London society in the twenties which comes from Daphne Fielding's *Mercury Presides* (London, 1954) or the first volume of Lady Diana Cooper's memoirs, *The Rainbow Comes and Goes* (London, 1958).[1] Anthony Powell's 'Music of Time' series similarly illuminates the higher society of the thirties and the changes of fortune in the war years. Waugh's purpose in *Vile Bodies* and *Decline and Fall* seems more nearly satirical; the historian should be always on guard not to accept any view of things from a novel as the gospel truth.

The historian of the thirties has much to quarry from, but he can also go deeper and seek the spirit of the age from the novelists. George Orwell's novels seem almost as much documentaries as *The Road to Wigan Pier*. *Coming up for Air* depicts the village engulfed by suburbia, *Keep the Aspidistra Flying* the seedy respectability of a class. Walter Greenwood's *Love on the Dole* (London, 1933) is remarkable for its portrayal not just of the working-class texture of 'Hankey Park', one of the poorer parts of Manchester, but of the psychology of the unemployed. Here is the 'means test' at the Labour Exchange, as experienced in the novel (p. 192).

> Hearing the man's indignant expostulations, a policeman, on duty at the door, came nearer, silently. The man, grey-haired, middle-aged, a stocky fellow in corduroys, clay-muddied blucher boots and with 'yorks' strapped about his knees, exclaimed: 'What d'you mean? Nothin' for me. I'm out o'collar, aren't I?'
>
> The clerk put aside his pen and sighed, wearily: 'Doan argue wi' me,' he appealed: "Tisn't my fault. If you want to know why, go'n

[1] Mrs Fielding was previously the Marchioness of Bath.

see the manager. Blimey, you blokes're blurry well drivin' me barmy this mornin'.'

'Manager, eh?' the man snapped: 'You bet I'll see the manager. Where is 'e?' The clerk jerked his thumb towards the far end of the counter. 'Ask at "Enquiries",' he said: 'Who's next?'

Harry followed the man.

The manager ordered a clerk to look up the man's particulars; the clerk handed over some documents after a search in a filing cabinet. His superior, after perusing some notes written upon the form, looked at the applicant and said: 'You've a couple of sons living with you who are working, haven't you?'

'Aye,' the man answered: 'One's earning twenty-five bob an' t'other a couple o' quid, when they work a full week. An' the eldest he's . . .'

'In view of this fact,' the manager interrupted: 'The Public Assistance Committee have ruled your household's aggregate income sufficient for your needs; therefore your claim for transitional benefit is disallowed. . . .'

The man flushed: 'The swine,' he shouted: 'Th' eldest lad's gettin' wed . . . 'as 'e to keep me an' the old woman?' Raising his fist: 'I'll . . .' But the attendant policeman collared him and propelled him outside, roughly, ignoring his loud protestations.

Beside this A. G. Macdonell's *England, their England* (London, 1933) seems almost flippant: an exploration of contemporary England by that useful fall guy, the Scotsman who finds his neighbours so strange. The village cricket match against J. C. Squire's team, the stockbroker's country golf club, the village pub, Tory electioneering in the 1931 election, the denizens of the London night clubs are all put upon the stage. Insight and entertainment are here hard to separate. And for the younger generation in the provinces in the thirties—meeting for coffee in the mornings or for adventures in thinking and in sexual relationships at the week-ends—where can one find the past encapsulated better than in William Cooper's *Scenes from Provincial Life* or the first of C. P. Snow's Lewis Elliott novels, *A Time of Hope*? And how is one to place, and to use, a chronicle of a family which re-creates the times of a whole generation, from the Edwardian age to the

1960s? This is what Angus Wilson has done, with an artist's or poet's inspiration, in *No Laughing Matter*.

One writer has caught the Londoner's life in the Second World War with supreme skill: Elizabeth Bowen. You must read her *Heat of the Day* to discover this, and perhaps even more her short stories, written during the war and collected as *The Demon Lover*. If one had to choose one of the stories, it should be 'Mysterious Kôr'. But read her postscript to the book to see why the stories have such force.

> During the war I lived, both as a civilian and as a writer, with every pore open; I lived so many lives, and, still more, lived among the packed repercussions of so many thousands of other lives, all under stress, that I see now it would have been impossible to have been writing only one book... Had it not been for my time to time promises to write stories, much that had been pressing against the door might have remained pressing against it in vain. I do not feel I 'invented' anything I wrote. It seemed to me that during the war the overcharged subconsciousnesses of everybody overflowed and merged. It is because the general subconsciousness saturates these stories that they have an authority nothing to do with me.
>
> These are all war-time, none of them *war* stories. There are no accounts of war action even as I knew it—for instance, air raids. Only one character—in 'Mysterious Kôr'—is a soldier; and he only appears as a homeless wanderer round a city. These are, more, studies of climate, and of the strange growths it raised...[1]

The absurdities of the war, and the nastiness of some of its episodes, as experienced by an older man, Guy Crouchback, are described in Evelyn Waugh's trilogy, *Sword of Honour* (London, 1965).[2] Anthony Powell's later novels take us through Nick Jenkins' war, showing the indiscriminate deaths which the Blitz inflicted and the languors of army life—a posting to Northern Ireland, Charles Stringham in the Mobile Laundry unit, Bithel,

[1] Elizabeth Bowen, *The Demon Lover* (London, 1945; collected edition 1952), 217.

[2] First published as *Men at Arms* (London, 1952), *Officers and Gentlemen* (London, 1955), *Unconditional Surrender* (London, 1961).

the 'small-town liar and misfit', and Biggs, the officer who hanged himself in the hut in the sports field. But to recapture London *after* the Blitz, and as it remained for four or five years, one must go to the opening passage of one of the peacetime novels, *Casanova's Chinese Restaurant.*

> Crossing the road by the bombed-out public house on the corner and pondering the mystery which dominates vistas framed by a ruined door, I felt for some reason glad the place had not yet been rebuilt. A direct hit had excised even the ground floor, so that the basement was revealed as a sunken garden, or site of archaeological excavation long abandoned, where great sprays of willow herb and ragwort flowered through cracked paving stones; only a few milk bottles and a laceless boot recalling contemporary life. In the midst of this sombre grotto five or six fractured steps had withstood the explosion and formed a projecting island of masonry on the summit of which rose the door. Walls on both sides were shrunk away, but along its lintel, in niggling copybook writing, could still be distinguished the word *Ladies.*[1]

When we come to the fifties and sixties the choice seems much larger because reputations have not yet been established or overthrown. Iris Murdoch's novels, when they are not timeless, reflect the permissive society, John Braine's *Room at the Top* the amoral young man on the make, unsure of his place but determined to improve it. Muriel Spark, Edna O'Brien, Kingsley Amis, Pamela Hansford Johnson—will their novels be used for quarries, or read as part of the Great Tradition, or simply be forgotten?

The poet, so Hoggart tells us, 'speaks more often [than the novelist] in his own person. His witness is more direct and contemporary.' He is much concerned with language and technique. At the highest, his poems are 'the very culture of the feelings'.[2] It would need a poet to select the poems of twentieth century poets which achieve this. At a lower level one turns to the time when poetry, life and politics seemed most closely intertwined, the

[1] Anthony Powell, *Casanova's Chinese Restaurant* (London, 1960; Penguin edition, 1964), 9.

[2] R. Hoggart, *loc. cit.*, 234–5.

thirties, particularly during the Spanish Civil War. Thus C. Day
Lewis' long epic, 'The Nabara', is often quoted:

> Freedom is more than a word, more than the base coinage
> Of statesmen, the tyrant's dishonoured cheque, or the dreamer's mad
> Inflated currency.

Similarly the verse plays by W. H. Auden and Christopher
Isherwood, *The Ascent of F.6* (London, 1936) and *The Dog Beneath
the Skin* (London, 1935), express the fears and boredom and dis-
illusion of the thirties. Here is part of a chorus from the latter:

> Hiker with sunburn blisters on your office pallor,
> Cross-country champion with corks in your hands,
> When you have eaten your sandwich, your salt and your apple,
> When you have begged your glass of milk from the ill-kept farm,
> What is it you see?
>
> I see barns falling, fences broken,
> Pasture not ploughland, weeds not wheat.
> The great houses remain but only half are inhabited,
> Dusty the gunrooms and the stable clocks stationary.
> Some have been turned into prep-schools, where the diet is in the
>   hands of an experienced matron,
> Others into club-houses for the golf-bore and the top-holes.
> Those who sang in the inns at evening have departed;
>   they saw their hope in another country,
> Their children have entered the service of the suburban areas;
>   they have become typists, mannequins and factory operatives;
>   they desired a different rhythm of life.
>
> But their places are taken by another population, with
>   views about nature,
> Brought in charabanc and saloon along arterial roads;
> Tourists to whom the Tudor cafés
> Offer Bovril and buns on Breton ware
> With leather work as a sideline; Filling stations
> Supplying petrol from rustic pumps.

Or take Day Lewis' poem of a night in the Home Guard,
'Watching Post', dated July 1940:

A hill flank overlooking the Axe valley.
Among the stubble a farmer and I keep watch
For whatever may come to injure our countryside—
Light signals, parachutes, bombs, or sea-invaders.
The moon looks over the hill's shoulder, and hope
Mans the old ramparts of an English night.

Of plays one well-known example must suffice. John Osborne's
Look Back in Anger (London, 1956) has been taken as representing
and preserving the 'angry young men' of the fifties. Jimmy
Porter, ex-working class, a university graduate who has married
Alison, a girl of a higher social class, can find no better occupation
than running a sweet stall. Alison says to her father, a retired army
officer, 'You're hurt because everything is changed. Jimmy is hurt
because everything is the same.' Another character says of Jimmy
that 'there's no place for people like him any longer—in sex or
politics or anything. That's why he's so futile. He was born out of
his time.'

There remains another area in which the student of literature
offers help, that of 'popular art, mass art and some other forms of
mass communication'. What this embraces makes quite a long list,
some of whose items need treatment in a separate chapter.
Hoggart's list includes 'advertisements, romantic novelettes,
cartoons and strip-cartoons, sex-and-violence novels, popular
song, the press, women's magazine fiction, radio and television,
film';[1] to which one should surely add a host of glossy magazines
designed for light reading or titillation, and boys', girls' and
children's magazines. Such materials help to 'define social and
cultural changes', but only if the critic is at hand to distinguish
what is peculiar to the author and what is representative and
topical.[2]

It will be seen that the uses of imaginative writing depend, as
has been said, very largely on the personal taste of the historian—
or, to be precise, on his emotional reaction to the emotions
recorded and reflected in the literature. To treat novels, plays and

[1] R. Hoggart, *loc. cit.*, 239.
[2] *Ibid.*, 245.

poems as 'sources' of the same kind as state papers or political correspondence not only does improper violence to the writers so exploited but begs questions which need more accurate answers. The classic case of such mishandling is provided by the Russian conviction that the novels of Charles Dickens may be used as a source for English social conditions in the nineteenth century. Yet Dickens was, within limits, a realistic novelist; the moderns, who have moved away from realism, clearly make such use even less suitable. Thus the historian may get the flavour of the Nottinghamshire mining community early in this century from D. H. Lawrence, or the feel of upper-class society between the wars from Anthony Powell. But he needs to go to very different sources if he is to understand the real social and economic circumstances of the first, or the political preconceptions of the second. All literature worthy of the name transmutes into art the experience which it is the historian's business to ascertain in fact, and it is arguable that to the historian the value of imaginative writing varies inversely with the quality of the writer. The more ordinary he is, the less transmuting does he apply; remarkable, unusual and very personal novelists and poets by their very qualities rise above and beyond the historian's methods of assessment, perhaps beyond his needs. However, the transmuted reality is also heightened: the greater the artist, the more he may (probably will) fill the mind with the means of appreciation. Thus the uses of literature to the historian are essentially preliminary and secondary: it equips him for the understanding of an age (and this is understanding he must acquire) and can give human identity to his facts and problems, but it does not supply the facts or solve the problems. The point is worth stating only because people sometimes try to give to literature the quality of direct evidence which it does not possess. The historian who writes about the Second World War without some acquaintance with Waugh's Crouchback will lack an important understanding of a significant and influential mentality; the historian who uses the experiences of Guy Crouchback instead of those of some actual officer evades his duty. A comparative study of Siegfried Sassoon's autobiography and its fictionalised version in *The Memoirs of a Fox-Hunting Man* might prove of interest in this connection.

4. NEWSPAPER AND OTHER PERIODICALS

Newspapers are, on the face of it, such a vital source for the historian of the twentieth century that we may seem to have been guilty of a dereliction of duty in not treating them much earlier. Of course they are important, in several different ways; but like the *Parliamentary Debates* their bulk is an obstacle and the gold content of their ore is low. The historian who sets out to reconstruct the history of even a single month from the newspapers would find himself engaged in a long and tedious task, going through page after page of not just one paper but half a dozen or more. If he uses bound copies, then the strain on his eyes, his neck (from peering now at the top, now at the bottom of the page) and his arms is great; if he is using a microfilm copy the strain on his eyes is even greater. In time perhaps he will discipline himself to look only at the headlines, and note down only a few passages from each issue; but he is always in danger of being tempted up by-ways or into a cul-de-sac, following some story, some trial, some matrimonial dispute which is entertaining but not a piece of history worth recording. In the end he must resort to sampling— with the danger of missing some essential grain of truth. You must know something about your subject to begin with, and have at least a rough idea of the main dates; you then know what to look for in the papers, and can wear blinkers to exclude everything else from your view. You cannot write history simply by reading several newspapers all through.[1]

Yet the newspaper has much to give the historian. First, the news itself: the atmosphere of a debate or a conference, a notice of an important but hitherto ignored meeting. About national events

[1] The main collection of newspapers in Great Britain is the British Museum's Newspaper Library at Colindale, which has the national papers (and also the weeklies) and many local newspapers, though some of its holdings were lost in the Second World War. Files of local newspapers are often available in local public libraries or record offices.

the researcher may find little in the papers which is not already
known to him, except that the press may add significant details;
but if his interest is local, the press is likely to be his only source of
information, for example about the course of an election campaign
in a particular town or constituency. More important than the
news, facts, information, may be the way in which the news was
presented, how it appeared to the public at the time. An example
is at hand from the Rising in Dublin on Easter Monday, 24 April
1916. All the news the reader of *The Times* received next day was
under the heading 'A raid on Ireland. German attempt to land
arms.' There was no full report until Thursday, 27 April, three
days after the insurrection had begun, and not until 1 May, when
the text of the Proclamation of the Republic was published, would
the reader have any idea what the Rising was about.[1] The government's panic reaction, the resort to martial law and the disastrous
executions by firing squads are the more understandable when the
lack of general information is realised (the government doubtless
knew more than the press, but not much more). Or again, the
build-up of the crisis in August 1931 which in a couple of weeks
toppled the Labour government must be studied in the press—the
shrill headlines, the tendentious editorials which helped to *make* the
crisis and were thus self-fulfilling. Indeed, news is often an active
force, something much more than simple information; the
medium is the message. How can one separate truth from wish,
the authentic from the shallowly impressionistic, in a news
report? Only by comparison with other reports, or with later,
perhaps less hasty, accounts in the weeklies or nearly contemporary books, or from a knowledge of this or that reporter or of
this paper's viewpoint.[2]

For one must also read the editorials. We may doubt how far
editorials influence opinion, or are read except for amusement;
but they do represent someone's thought about the news, and they

[1] See my article, 'The Irish Question in British Politics (1916–1922)' in *The Irish Struggle 1916–1926*, ed. Desmond Williams (London, 1966).
[2] For an analysis of different newspapers' contents in 1961 see Raymond Williams, *Britain in the Sixties: Communications* (London, 1962).

may have more sense of perspective than a correspondent's report. Editorials are important for recapturing the unfolding story, the mounting excitement or fear on the part of the public, the day-by-day impact of the news of, for instance, the Munich crisis in 1938. Geoffrey Dawson's alterations in a *Times* 'leader', suggesting on 7 September a simple surrender of territory by the Czechs, may have contributed to the crisis (Dawson was believed to express official policy more than was quite the case).[1] Earlier, *The Times'* ridicule of a suggested outlet to the sea for Abyssinia as a 'corridor for camels' (16 December 1935) may have helped to kill the 'Hoare-Laval deal' for a settlement of the Italian-Abyssinian war. It is possible, from a study of editorials and the tone of news reports (but one needs also to know what was being suppressed or slanted), to follow a newspaper's campaign or long-range policy. This is most easily done for *The Times*, whose official history was extremely critical of the policies of Dawson (the editor) in the 'appeasement' era—policies which led to some resignations from its staff.[2] A more favourable view of *The Times* is gained from seeing the part it played in criticising the government's intransigent war policy towards Ireland in 1921 and helping (along with many other influences) to bring about the truce and the eventual treaty.[3]

Allied to editorials are the correspondence columns and the cartoons. The former can, at the least, give a worm's-eye view of current events and prejudices as discerned by the reader with an urge to express his views. Probably only letters to *The Times* have a chance of starting some campaign or building up 'public opinion' to the point that government feels obliged to yield or to compromise (or perhaps simply to dig in its toes); for here pontificate the self-chosen men of influence and the chief public figures of the day. It is equally hard to judge the effect of cartoons. They

[1] Harold Nicolson's *Diaries and Letters 1930–1939* (very good for the day-by-day recall of the Munich crisis) suggest that Dawson did not alter this editorial: p. 358. See also Evelyn Wrench, *Geoffrey Dawson and our Times* (London, 1955).

[2] *History of The Times*, IV, Part 2 (London, 1952), 941, 945.

[3] *Ibid.*, 553–77.

express a view, they amuse, they make excellent illustrations for a book of history, giving an instantaneous comment on events. The best known for much of the century were David Low's in the *Evening Standard*, and they are easily studied because they were collected and published: e.g., *Years of Wrath: a cartoon history 1932–1945* (London, 1949). Osbert Lancaster's *'Maudie'* in the *Daily Express*, Vicky in the *New Statesman* and *Evening Standard* in the fifties, Giles in the *Sunday Express* have been much admired in their day.

This leaves us with 'features', gossip column, cheesecake, sex and scandal stories, pictures and advertisements. These may seem to concern chiefly the social historians and the historians of morals, dress and fashion. Reviews of books, plays and films help to establish or change standards of taste and criticism. The historian seeking to discover when central heating became commonplace in middle-class houses may have to resort to the newspaper advertisements of the sixties for his data.

There remains the question of a newspaper's affiliations, its political complexion. Some knowledge of newspaper history may be necessary if a paper's news and views are to be interpreted correctly. Those who have grown up with today's papers may feel that they know what they need to know about them already; but the recent past is littered with dead newspapers, and others have changed their tune, or even their name.[1]

Of the London morning papers *The Times* claims pride of place, 'the newspaper as an institution' as it has been called. Nominally independent, it has always been of 'the Establishment' and its independent support of the government of the day has been warmer towards a Conservative government than to its rivals. When Lord Northcliffe owned it (to his death in 1922) he largely left policy to the editors, Dawson (1912–19) and Wickham

[1] The *Report* of the Royal Commission on the Press 1947–49 (Cmd. 7700: 1949) and Harold Herd, *The March of Journalism* (London, 1952) are two none-too-recent authorities. For an analysis of the Press in 1961 see Raymond Williams, *Britain in the Sixties: Communications* (London, 1962), especially 46–54. For current information see *Willing's Press Guide* (annual).

Steed, the latter a distinguished student of foreign affairs whose viewpoint was independent and liberal. After Northcliffe's death the paper was owned by J. J. Astor and the Walter family (the original proprietors) until bought by Lord Thomson of Fleet in 1966. Astor restored the ineffable Dawson, an imperialist, a squire, a Fellow of All Souls and a frequenter of Cliveden, who knew little of Europe, to the editorial chair, which he kept till 1941, but his deputy and successor, R. Barrington-Ward, became more liberal in his views during the war. The long reign of Sir William Haley as editor was from 1952 to 1966. Under him *The Times* was correct, at times preachey. It also, for once, fell out with the Conservative Party.

Most other London papers have been as consistent. The *Daily Telegraph* can be relied on to be Conservative, the *Manchester Guardian* (after 1959 the *Guardian*) to be Liberal, or perhaps one should say liberal, for under the great C. P. Scott (to 1932) and his successors it has always followed an independent line. The *Daily Chronicle* and the *Daily News*, both Liberal, joined to become the *News Chronicle* in 1930; it expired in 1960. The *Morning Post*, die-hard Tory, died in 1937. The *Daily Express* was always a popular paper aiming at a mass circulation. Lord Beaverbrook, its owner, kept close control over its staff and policy and made it the vehicle for his long and ineffectual campaign for Empire Free Trade. The *Daily Mail*, which Northcliffe had founded in 1896 as the first paper aiming at the new mass-market, retained its popular and patriotic flavour under Northcliffe's brother, Lord Rothermere, and his successors. Of the *Daily Sketch* and the *Daily Mirror*, the latter began the spectacular ascent to its five-million circulation during the Second World War, when under its editor, Hugh Cudlipp, it became the liberal-minded champion of the people, often supporting Labour.[1] The *Daily Herald*, Labour's own paper (a weekly during the war of 1914–8), was taken over by Odhams Press in 1929, though the T.U.C. retained some control over its policy. In 1964 it was rescued by the International Publishing Corporation (the vehicle of the old

[1] See Hugh Cudlipp's book about it, *Publish and Be Damned* (London, 1953).

Rothermere interest) and renamed *The Sun*; in 1969 it was taken over by Rupert Murdoch, the Australian newspaper proprietor who had recently acquired control of the *News of the World*, and its politics (if any) are at present obscure. The *Financial Times'* popularity as more than just a business paper dates from the early sixties.

Of course London is not 'the whole bloody world' of the British press.[1] There are important provincial papers like the *Birmingham Post* and the *Yorkshire Post*. Scotland has the *Scotsman* and the *Glasgow Herald*. Wales has the *Western Mail* (Cardiff) and the *Liverpool Daily Post*. Many large cities have their own evening paper; the counties and many towns have their local weekly paper.

In many ways the weeklies are more useful and manageable for the historian. This category includes the Sunday papers which, even before their introduction of the colour magazine supplement in the sixties, were more like magazines than newspapers. Of the 'quality' Sundays the *Observer* deserves attention under its domineering editor J. L. Garvin (1908–42) with his formidable three-decker editorials. *Reynolds' News*, owned by the Co-operative movement, became the *Sunday Citizen* in 1962. The *People* and the *News of the World* were more popular, sensational and non-political. But it is not with these that most historians are likely to be concerned.

The weeklies are usable because they are somewhat more reflective than the dailies. One goes to them for views, not news. You can work through a volume of one far more quickly than through a year's file of a newspaper, and there will probably be an index. The weeklies have changed little in tone over the years. The *New Statesman* has remained independently socialist, exasperating and bitchy; its great editor (1930–60), Kingsley Martin, has written of his tenure of office in his autobiography, *Editor* (London, 1968). The *Spectator* has always been independently conservative. *Time*

[1] British recruit in Canada in the First World War gave his birthplace as London. *Officer:* London Ontario or London England? *Recruit:* London the whole bloody world (D. W. Brogan).

and Tide, so independently liberal that at times it became die-hard conservative, was started by Lady Rhondda in 1920. *Tribune* began its career as Labour's gadfly in 1937. *The Nation*, the great Liberal weekly under H. W. Massingham (editor till 1923) was absorbed by the *New Statesman* in 1931; much of J. M. Keynes' writing appeared in it in the twenties. Probably *The Economist* is more important throughout than any of these, though it was more strictly confined by its title before the 1950s. *Punch* for *Punch* and its political cartoons, the *Tablet* for Roman Catholic opinion, the *British Weekly* for nonconformity (Lloyd George accorded much respect to it and its editor until his death in 1923, Sir William Robertson Nicoll), the *Illustrated London News* for illustrations, *John Bull*, the poor man's false guardian while Horatio Bottomley ran it: all may have their uses, depending on the historian's tastes and interests.

Does anyone read the monthlies now, or the *Quarterly Review*, or do they survive on library and club subscriptions? The *Contemporary Review* was long edited by the eminent liberal historian G. P. Gooch. The *Twentieth Century* had once been the *Nineteenth Century*. The *Fortnightly* became a monthly and was absorbed by the *Contemporary* in 1934. The *National Review* under Leo Maxse purveyed an individual brand of Toryism during the First World War and afterwards was so extreme as to be ludicrous but for the fact that it had (presumably) some readers: Colonel Blimp would have seemed rose-pink by comparison. The *Round Table*, a quarterly, was founded before the First World War by members of Milner's 'kindergarten' to propagate their liberal imperialist views. Its tone was sane and bland; it published useful reports on events in Britain and in the different parts of the British Commonwealth in each issue, along with articles along the general lines of its interest. The *Political Quarterly*, founded in 1931 and edited by Professor W. A. Robson and Leonard Woolf, provided articles which discussed current questions in a balanced and liberal-minded way.

CHAPTER 6

Images, Sounds and Objects

For any period of history there is a large body of non-documentary sources to be considered, but the amount is exceptionally large for twentieth-century history: such very informative things as films, photographs, drawings and paintings, radio and television, sound recordings, interviews, objects preserved in museums, architecture and history-on-the-ground. Nor is this list exhaustive.

I. FILM

People concerned with the preservation of films have been arguing in recent years that their medium has a great deal to offer the historian, whom they blame for holding back from the feast because of his old-fashioned and conservative attitudes and his absorption in his conventional sources. There are, as we shall see, good reasons for scepticism on the historian's part. He is, however, becoming interested, though one must not exaggerate the number who are even in the pre-conversion stage. The University Historians' Film Committee was formed in 1968, the Film Committee of the Historical Association in 1969. Conferences at University College, London, called by Professor Thorold Dickinson, head of the Slade Film Department of the College, brought historians and film people together in April 1968 and September 1969. The proceedings of the former were published as *Film and the Historian* by the British Universities' Film Council. The B.U.F.C.'s journal, *University Vision*, had already devoted its first number (February 1968) to the historian and films. Six universities (Leeds, Nottingham, Reading, Edinburgh, Birmingham, Wales) formed in 1968 a consortium to make short films for use in teaching history.

Before the use of film as a historical source can be considered, several distinctions (not always clearly drawn) must be made between different uses which historians may make of films. There are at least six, and only the last falls within the scope of this book. They are:

(1) Films used for studying the history of film.

(2) Non-fiction films used for teaching or entertainment, particularly those called compilation films, using newsreel material, stills, maps and diagrams, specially shot scenes and re-enactments, and commentary. The line between films made for teaching and those made for entertainment is thin; films shown on television such as *The Great War* or *The Lost Peace* or *The Life and Times of Lord Mountbatten* were made to entertain first, though not without much care being taken over accuracy; the university consortium's film on *The Munich Crisis* was made first for teaching.[1]

(3) Films used for 'a form of instant briefing' of a historian on a subject. It is suggested, for example, that films of air raids taken by bomber crews during the Second World War would show the historian in a couple of hours the difficulties of crews in identifying targets and assessing damage—knowledge which it would take him days to reach in reading or work in the archives.[2]

(4) Films used as a form of historical publication. It is suggested that the making by a historian of 'film lectures, television film memoirs or academic historical documentaries' should be considered equivalent to publishing a book.[3] And, indeed, it may well be that the film, the cassette, the tape in a computer will become the medium for the publication of works of historical scholarship in the future.

(5) An archive of films designed as a complete repository of historical source material for the future. 'A planned cinematographic preservation of the whole range of human activity and the unravelling of political, economic, administrative and social events is as appropriate to this era as sound archives were to the world after the invasion of

---

[1] There are, of course, hundreds of films made commercially for teaching all subjects at all levels: see *Films for Universities* (London, 1969), a catalogue issued by the British Universities' Film Council.

[2] C. H. Roads, 'Film and the Historian', a paper delivered at the Library of Congress, Washington, 17 May 1969 (Imperial War Museum), 7.

[3] *Ibid.*, 9.

Images, Sounds and Objects

the radio or the printed or written word to centuries previous to the present.'[1]
(6) Existing films used as source material by the historian.

It is only with the last of these that we are here concerned.

That films must have some value as historical sources needs no argument. There are, however, many difficulties. Where are films to be found?[2] The National Film Archive, part of the British Film Institute, collects and preserves films, fiction and non-fiction. It selects films for preservation, but is dependent on the kindness of producers for the films it actually receives. There are facilities for viewing films at the Archive, but only a very few researchers can be accommodated at a time. The other great collection of film in Britain, and the oldest, is at the Imperial War Museum; it covers the two world wars of this century, and includes much foreign film and some material (for example, on Nazi Germany) of the inter-war years. Two newsreel companies, Visnews and Pathé, have extensive film archives. Several government departments have film archives, not always catalogued or usable; several industrial firms, such as Shell, and nationalised bodies such as the Coal Board and British Railways, have films of their own. The B.B.C. has its own film archive for its television services. The government maintains a Central Film Library in London, with equivalent libraries in Glasgow and Cardiff (for hiring out films).

What is there to be found in film? Everything or nothing: the trouble is that there is nothing for film on the scale of the bibliographies, catalogues, registers and indexes which exist for written sources; there is no equivalent to the National Register of Archives. The National Film Archive catalogues its films on cards, and has issued three printed catalogues of part of its holdings.[3] Since 1963 the British Industrial and Scientific Film

[1] *Ibid.*, 1.
[2] See the article by Sir Arthur Elton, 'The Film as Source Material for History', *Aslib Proceedings*, VII, 207–39 (November, 1955).
[3] National Film Archive, *Catalogue*, Part I, *Silent News Films 1895–1933* (London, 1951, second edition, 1965); Part II, *Silent Non-Fiction Films 1895–1934* (London, 1960); Part III, *Silent Fiction Films 1895–1930* (London, 1966).

165

Association has issued quarterly the *British National Film Catalogue* (cumulated into annual editions). Every repository of films presumably has some catalogue—the newsreel companies very full ones, for their collections are continually in commercial use; but the conventions of cataloguing are not fully established. The Imperial War Museum is now inaugurating a system of cataloguing its holdings in depth linked to a computerised high-speed retrieval system by which 'we will be able to locate very rapidly film shot of a specified street at a specified date' in Baghdad[1] (fifteen years ago the I.W.M. collection of film totalled 12 million feet).[2] A random page of the N.F.A. *Catalogue* of *Silent News Film* (p. 220) for part of 1925 is as follows (only the first entry is here given in full):

June 7

THE 'GORDON BENNETT', START OF THE WORLD'S MOST FAMOUS BALLOON RACE FROM SOLSBOSCH, BELGIUM (8).[3] Long shot of the competing balloons (20) medium close shot of the base of a balloon (25); 'ELSIE', BRITAIN (CENTRE), MET WITH DISASTER (3); medium close shot of three balloons including Elsie (36). CAPT. C. SPENCER IN 'MIRAMER' (40). Close-up of him and his wife? (50). Competing balloons, one airborne (55). Base of another balloon just starting (72).
TOPICAL BUDGET

June 28

(IN VICKERS AIRCRAFT.) THEIR MAJESTIES, THE KING AND QUEEN, WITH THE DUKE AND DUCHESS OF YORK, INSPECTING THE VICKERS 'VANGUARD'. ROYAL AIR FORCE DISPLAY, 1925.

July 1

100 YEARS OF RAILWAYS: DUKE OF YORK AT DARLINGTON CENTENARY CELEBRATIONS.
TOPICAL BUDGET

July 2

WONDERFUL AIRMANSHIP AT HENDON: THE ROYAL FAMILY WITNESS THRILLING EVOLUTION IN THE AIR AT THE R.A.F. PAGEANT.
GAUMONT. Serial No. 1490.

[1] Roads, *loc. cit.*, 13.
[2] Sir Arthur Elton, *loc. cit.*, 226.
[3] The numbers indicate film footage.

July 6
CATHOLIC POLICE WHO FELL IN WAR: BRIG:-GEN. SIR WILLIAM HORWOOD,
CHIEF COMMISSIONER, ATTENDS 3RD ANNUAL WESTMINSTER REQUIEM.
TOPICAL BUDGET. Serial No. 724-1

July 11
LONDON'S FIRE FIGHTERS: INSPECTION BY LORD JELLICOE AT VICTORIA
PARK.
TOPICAL BUDGET

July 27
'DAVENTRY CALLING . . . WIND AND RAIN AGAINST MY VOICES FIGHT IN
VAIN': POSTMASTER-GENERAL OPENS '5XX', THE WORLD'S GREATEST
BROADCASTING STATION.
TOPICAL BUDGET

Even to know where you might find films useful to you is not
enough to ensure success. 'Film, at present, is like the chained
Bible of the twentieth century: costly to reproduce and inaccessible to all but a privileged few for consultation at their own will.'[1]
Films at the National Film Archive and elsewhere can be viewed
at a viewing-table (where hundreds of feet can be rapidly run
through till one comes to shots of interest). To copy films (make
duplicate prints) is expensive, and public screenings are often
prohibited by copyright restrictions. Screening or the use of the
viewing-table involves payment to a projectionist. However, one
should not despair. The Slade Film Department of University
College, London, is now engaged, with the help of a grant from
the Social Science Research Council, in a project for discovering
and listing on index cards material on film and other audio-visual
media useful for historical research and teaching, particularly in
the period between the end of the N.F.A. *Catalogue* (London,
1933) and the start of the *British National Film Catalogue* (London,
1963). If some sort of central register of film comparable to the
National Register of Archives can be compiled, at least the
researcher will have a single source of information as to what is

[1] Lisa Pontecorvo, 'Film Archives and University Research', *University
Vision*, I, 27 (February 1968).

available and where; improved facilities for viewing and inspecting and copying might be expected to follow.

But how much will it be worth to the historian to pursue his researches into film material? There are dangers in the indiscriminate use of film to establish historical events or scenes, dangers perhaps no greater than in the use of any sources without proper criticism but to some extent peculiar to the nature of the medium. There are several kinds of film, but only one which is likely to be heavily used by historians. The fiction film, 'today's folklore', can give 'the popular attitude towards life',[1] the feel of the times, looks, dress, houses, manners, style of life. The technical film, made for instructional, advertising or promotional purposes, can preserve details of machinery and manufacturing methods which may otherwise be lost, though commercial photographs are another source for this. The propaganda film can be studied for its propaganda or for the feeling of the times, but it will portray actual scenes and events, though parts may be re-enactments or actuality material out of period or sequence. Thus British wartime films such as *Desert Victory* (1943) or *The True Glory* (1945) cannot be taken at face value. Film experts can give numerous examples; here are two. Two films, a German, *Baptism of Fire* (1939) and an American, *Why We Fight* (1941), used the same shots of the invasion of Poland but with reverse effects.[2] German government films ostensibly shot during the First World War came from a film, *Westfront 1918*, made in 1930.[3] Documentaries, though obviously useful as reports and as evidence of points of view, are again unlikely to escape a propaganda or hortatory character.

This leaves newsreels, which should be of prime interest to the historian, but in which the pitfalls are much more serious and harder to avoid. First, as with the other kinds of film, the date of the shots must be established. Where the cameraman's 'dope sheets' are available this is simplified and the problem of identifying the subjects of shots also; but usually this source is lacking.

[1] Sir Arthur Elton, *loc. cit.*, 208.
[2] Thorold Dickinson in *The Listener*, 15 May 1969.
[3] Paul Rotha in *The Listener*, 8 May 1969.

Actual film forgeries seem to be few.[1] But no newsreel is straight reporting. It has been cut and edited—a series like the *March of Time*, popular in the thirties, in particular. Scenes may be wrongly juxtaposed.[2] A good film archive would preserve all the 'cuts and overs' and stock shots—the surplus shots taken and never used in the newsreels. When all else is allowed for there remains the problem of bias, conscious or unconscious. *The Munich Crisis* has been criticised[3] for showing street scenes in London with crowds cheering Chamberlain and not the counter-demonstrations in Trafalgar Square (were they filmed?). Cameramen in the Spanish Civil War found that most newspapers and newsreels would not print shots showing the German origin of Nationalist aeroplanes.[4]

So in using material from the millions of feet of newsreels the historian must not only know what he is looking for, find good catalogues, and have hours to spend at the viewing-table, but must also discover the provenance, location, distributor of whatever newsreels he uses, and if possible the much greater bulk of the surplus shots also. Some kinds of film (not strictly newsreels) are much more reliable than others. In the Second World War bomber and fighter crews made 16 mm camera gun films of raids (these cameras were fitted into the bellies of bombers and the noses of fighters) and were instructed to 'get coverage', i.e., film everything they saw.[5] Anything else will have been excerpted, edited, and the surplus shots probably not preserved.

And what evidence for his work will the historian be getting who has overcome all the hazards of inaccessibility, lack of time and technical obscurity in using film material? He can see things as they actually were. Just press the button and the camera will show everything in front of it (but here the *aim* is all-important, as well as 'being there'). Film, especially newsreels, will give him the feel of the times, the character of society, a sense of concrete

[1] Sir Arthur Elton, *loc. cit.*, 207n.
[2] Pontecorvo, *loc. cit.*, 3L; Sir Arthur Elton, *loc. cit.*, 212–16.
[3] A. J. P. Taylor in *Film and the Historian*, 10.
[4] Thorold Dickinson, *ibid.*, 10–11.
[5] Sir Arthur Elton, *loc. cit.*, 216. Cf. Roads, *loc. cit.*, 2.

reality, of immediacy and scale. The magnetism of a speaker can be captured, or the high moments of a ceremony such as the Coronation in 1953.[1] The newsreel or the stock shots can correct the views put out by propaganda—film serving as corrective to film. It boils down (may one suggest?) to telling the historian about happenings, propaganda, technology, war. Is it the accident of the Imperial War Museum's incomparable holdings that the scanty literature of the subject seems to find most of its examples from war? For more mundane subjects perhaps even the twentieth-century historian may for a while yet stick to his traditional sources in the written or printed word. And, beyond that, why not photographs?

2. PHOTOGRAPHS, PICTURES

Photographs of persons, events, ceremonies, buildings, streets, villages, landscape, aerial photographs can tell the historian much; indeed, all except the last have been available for well over a century. They are more commonly used for illustration than for research. Photographs of politicians are perhaps most frequently reproduced, and the danger is that they may tempt people into forms of amateur psychology more entertaining than useful. Moreover, one cannot always trust the attributions, particularly in a group photograph, and even more one cannot trust the dating of photographs (if, indeed, it is given at all). Countess Lloyd-George had to write to the *Observer* pointing out that the caption to a photo of a Lloyd George family picnic which identified her as in the group was incorrect.[2] Several pictures of Baldwin as a boy, youth and young man, reproduced in Barnes and Middlemas, *Baldwin*, are wrong as to his age. It is essential that the date of a photograph be given, particularly for quickly ageing politicians; but it often is not. Photographs of towns during the depression of the thirties are rarely reproduced: Jarrow, a place in the Rhondda,

[1] Sir Arthur Elton, *loc. cit.*, 208–11; Roads, *loc. cit.*, 4–8.
[2] *Observer*, 8 December 1968, referring to picture in the Colour Magazine for 17 November.

Workington. If they were, we would need to know the time of
year, the time of day and the weather when the picture was taken.
Almost anywhere can look miserable on a dark rainy afternoon;
and a clever photographer who 'poses' his picture and selects the
best time for light and shadow can make an idyll out of a very
commonplace street. Photographs of battle scenes, the trenches,
wounded soldiers, a shell-scarred village street can be authentic
but lend themselves to treatment for propaganda purposes; and,
again, one must be sure that captions and pictures correspond.
Pictures of towns, streets, buildings in peacetime may usually be a
more reliable record than those taken in the press of war. It will
be particularly important for the future historian to have 'before
and after' pictures of places that have been rebuilt and redeve-
loped; even the old street plan may go if the bombers or the
developers are sufficiently ruthless. Changes can now occur very
quickly: a familiar building, an old toll house, a railway station
can be razed overnight; recently it is not only closed stations—
large urban terminals as well as country stations—which have been
demolished, but stations still open, where in the interest of
economy the commodious old building is replaced by a steel-and-
glass bus shelter. The new Euston station in London has
completely obliterated the old.

There must be a huge mass of photographic material in private
hands, and to think of a national catalogue of such material is
impossible. Newspapers may have large collections of photographs, used and unused, in their files. The Imperial War Museum
has 'more than $3\frac{1}{2}$ million prints and negatives' on the two world
wars. The largest general collection is the Radio Times Hulton
Picture Library, owned by the B.B.C., and based partly on the
collection of *Picture Post*, the former weekly which started it in
1938; it is not available for research. The National Portrait
Gallery has the National Portrait Record of the great and near-
great, since 1917, which can be seen by arrangement.[1] Pictures of
bombed buildings, particularly buildings of historical or archi-

[1] Information from section on *Photographs* in the bibliography of A. J. P.
Taylor, *English History 1914–1945* (Oxford, 1965), 609–10.

tectural interest, were kept by an official body, the National Buildings Record, from 1940 onwards; there is now the more general National Monuments Record. Several county record offices have collections of photographs of places and persons.

Drawings and paintings can also capture the spirit of a man or woman, a street or a battle scene. The line between art and record may be difficult to draw. There were official war artists in both wars; most of their works are in the Imperial War Museum. The National Portrait Gallery includes many twentieth-century subjects.

3. SOUND RECORDS

Radio and television broadcasting have obviously produced a vast amount of material recorded on discs or tapes, though most of this is doubtless not retained for long. Here again one must distinguish between sound records (whether the B.B.C.'s or the record companies') which illustrate the history of serious music, or jazz and other forms of popular music and entertainment, or the history of speech and dialect, and records used for the more general study of history. A record can give you the sound of a speaker's voice, his style and pace and perhaps effect (cheers or hisses); but you must be sure the record's attribution of the speaker is correct, and you need to know the date of the speech. For the actual text a printed version is more reliable, though recorded and printed versions might well be compared. Neither is necessarily authentic; and the recorded text, which may be edited or even completely distorted by cutting and splicing, is more dangerous to use than the printed version. It is quite possible to edit the tape of a speech to make the speaker say the direct opposite of what he actually said. Again, the main collection is the B.B.C. Sound Archives, which are not open to the public, though the B.B.C. is at present considering how to make the use of it available for educational purposes, both for teaching and research. The British Institute of Recorded Sound has a large and growing collection of records, including recordings of B.B.C. broadcasts. It is beginning to compile a register of archives of recordings. It operates a free listening service for serious students.[1] There are records on sale of Churchill's speeches and of the voices of other politicians and poets—and also of the sounds of steam locomotives at work.

4. INTERVIEWS

The tape-recorder comes into use again in connection with interviews, which can be an important source for the twentieth-century historian. There are plenty of survivors from the beginning of the century and earlier, and to use their evidence is an advantage which the 'contemporary historian' in any age has over his successors. Nowadays, with a small portable tape-recorder, the interviewer can get the actual words exchanged at the interview and need not rely on his memory or his speed in note-taking; however, being recorded may prove inhibiting to the person being interviewed. In the United States projects for oral history are commonplace—successors to the many reminiscences of frontiersmen and pioneers compiled by interview by Western state and county historical societies. In this country at least one memoir has been made in this way: Francis Williams' compilation of Lord Attlee's reminiscences, *A Prime Minister Remembers* (London, 1961). Nuffield College is assembling archives of the memories, letters and papers of recent politicians: the diary of G. R. Strauss, M.P., has been tape-recorded for this archive.

Much interviewing is less ambitious. It may consist of a series of conversations with a retired politician, and questions put to him; historians working on the Baldwin era have found Lord Davidson (J. C. C. Davidson, Baldwin's friend and confidant, who was in Parliament in the twenties and thirties) a valuable source in this way; his own memoirs have now been published.[2] Often the subject studied and the man interviewed are more limited. Researchers have been able to tap a rich vein of memories of trade union officials, leaders of the unemployed, Labour men in

[1] The B.I.R.S. office is at 29 Exhibition Road, London S.W.7.
[2] See above, p. 109.

politics or local government, by means of interviews. Advertisements in local newspapers may uncover persons willing to be interviewed; and the result may also be the loan of valuable and hitherto unknown minutes and records of societies or unions, their publications and other ephemera. Indeed, an interview may well lead to the preservation in a library of material otherwise at risk of loss or destruction at any time.[1]

The hazards of the interview are obvious enough. Many of the normal tests to which all evidence should be submitted must be applied. How sound is the memory of the man or woman? Can his or her statements be supported by documentary evidence—letters, a diary, papers? Do his statements check with evidence from other sources? *Was he there?* And has he prepared for the interview, or is he perforce answering off the cuff, reaching back far into his memory for things not thought of for many years?

Interviewing needs a technique of its own. The interviewer must know a good deal about the subject, and the person to be interviewed, beforehand. He must have decided what questions to ask—though ready to be led off into fruitful digressions if they occur. He must know when to prompt his informant with references to events or to other persons he might have known in order to jog his memory. And, unless he is using a tape-recorder, he must decide whether to take notes during the interview, which may prove distracting to both parties and interrupt the flow of memory, or to rely on his own memory and make notes as soon as possible afterwards. Whatever course is followed, he may need to come back for a second session, to check what has already been put down; or it may be possible to get an agreed record of the interview by correspondence.

These are the basic technicalities of 'oral history'—history taken from the horse's mouth. They resemble, of course, the problems raised by memoirs, for whether a man is putting his reminiscences on paper or on tape makes no fundamental difference. But the collection of evidence by interview does have some

[1] For interviews of Labour personalities see the *Bulletin of the Society for the Study of Labour History.*

features peculiar to itself. There are obvious advantages: some memoirs thus get preserved that might never have been written, and the interpolation of questions can extract information which the subject might have omitted unprompted. Also, the interviewer, if alert enough, can immediately assess, to some extent at least, the reliability of what he is told from such things as tone of voice, facial expression or hesitations. Conversely, he has to be on his guard not to evoke false facts or emphases by his very questions, or to read his subjective impressions of the occasion too readily into the record. There are, however, two quite serious drawbacks to which attention might be directed. Tape-recordings are in a sense privileged evidence in a way in which the printed book, available to all and open to free assessment, is not. The interviewer is on his honour to use the matter obtained correctly, and he is also obliged to respect the feelings of the person interviewed. This inhibits use and especially inhibits searching criticism. Secondly, the person interviewed is not on oath and cannot readily produce his evidence; his opinions, in particular, carry only the weight of his personality, not that of considered and documented study. Thus it seems likely that this kind of material is, for the present, most useful in supplying what one may call chronicle-type evidence: facts, events, anecdotes, occasionally character sketches. It is, actually, not easy so far to know how such recorded evidence should be used and assessed. The few historians who have employed it have, quite rightly, absorbed it into their general account, and the occasional footnote explaining that the information was obtained in this way does not make considered assessment of the technique possible. We neeed a proper analytical study of the subject.

5. MUSEUMS

Museums may at first blush seem unlikely to contain much about the twentieth century. Of course any art gallery will have paintings and sculpture of the century, and even of very recent years; one thinks of the Tate Gallery, but every good gallery in the provinces will have examples. Museums only look unpromising to those who think they contain nothing but stuffed birds, butterflies, prehistoric skeletons and suits of armour. A visit to the Science Museum in South Kensington is a quick enlightenment. Here are machines or models of the very latest designs, in electricity, telecommunications, steel-making, textiles, mining, chemicals, transport, roads and bridges, photography, nuclear power, navigation. There is a model of a space rocket engine. The historian of the motor car will find the first Austin Seven (1922) and a Rover gas turbine car of 1950, and several models in between; the railway historian can see the Great Western Railway locomotive of the twenties, 'Caerphilly Castle' and a 'Deltic' diesel engine as well as an Underground carriage of the 1927 series and modern signalling apparatus; there is also a Glasgow Corporation tramcar. The aeronautics section contains early gliders and R.A.F. planes and later planes including the Hawker Hurricane, the Spitfire and the Gloster jet aircraft. The recent history of railway locomotives and rolling-stock, and London trams and buses, is also to be seen at the Transport Museum at Clapham, which has a galaxy of preserved exhibits; and there are the other railway museums at York and Swindon and several enthusiasts' preservation centres, as well as examples of this or that twentieth-century locomotive stored away by some preservation society or privately owned.

Several provincial museums (Birmingham and Leicester are two) have recently taken over steam locomotives for exhibition, and Birmingham has a particularly fine museum of industrial technology. The National Museum of Wales has a splendid section of industrial archaeology, with models of modern mining practice, oil refineries, steamships and electrical equipment. Indeed, the museum-lover could doubtless compile a long list of museums up and down the country, both municipal and private, with twentieth-century material; for example, specialised museums of automobiles and aircraft. Even an unlikely candidate, the Victoria and Albert, has a collection of women's fashions ending with wartime utility clothes and a Dior model of 1947, and a series of fashion plates coming down to 1950. The Geffrye Museum in Shoreditch has furniture and domestic equipment reaching to the present day. The Imperial War Museum has been mentioned so often already that further reference to its great holdings is unnecessary. The historian who wants to see modern artifacts of any sort will find a museum to suit him;[1] alternatively, he can go and see these things on the ground.

6. HISTORY ON THE GROUND

Field-work will seem another unlikely resource for the twentieth-century historian; and if he resorts to it he will probably find himself footsore from pounding city pavements rather than cursing his muddy boots. It is a truism that much of the country is changing fast—hedges being grubbed up, fields thrown together, bare hillsides afforested, land cut across by motorways or road widenings. Most villages have their new houses, and every town and city has grown outward, the latter upward as well. Photographs, including aerial photographs, can often tell a good deal, particularly those 'before and after'; indeed, to see a landscape or townscape today and not know what it was like ten, twenty, fifty years ago will not help in historical reconstruction at all.

Maps can tell a good deal. However, the one-inch ordnance survey maps in commonest use must be treated with caution; many now in use are dated 1952, with some later changes, or 1966; the latest adds 'reprinted with the addition of new major roads 1969'. Road changes, expansion of built-up areas, and railways and stations closed may not be shown clearly on the one-inch maps, and even if they are the dating leaves a good deal of leeway. The tracks of railways which have had their rails taken up are shown by thin dotted lines, over- and under-bridges and cuttings; but these soon disappear in areas of new building. A series of dated one-inch maps going back over half a century is obviously more helpful; better still are the $2\frac{1}{2}$-inch, 6-inch or 25-inch sheets

---

[1] *Museums and Galleries in Great Britain and Northern Ireland* (Index Publication); *Guide to London Museums and Galleries* (H.M.S.O.).

going back several years. A recent 2½-inch sheet reads 'made and published 1956. Reprinted with minor corrections 1960 . . . compiled from 6 sheets last fully revised 1911–14. Other partial systematic revision 1938–51 has been incorporated.'

With or without a map, what can the historian find on the ground? Visits to factories at work can tell him more about modern industry than scores of photographs or films, can give him the feel of things. Modern architecture needs to be seen, and not necessarily on a bright, sunny day. South London has been transformed by tower blocks of flats, making a new skyscape amid the miles of streets. The central London vista has been transformed by the office blocks that almost dwarf St Paul's or the Houses of Parliament. Layers of history can be seen around London, Manchester, Bristol, any large city, with council housing estates of successive dates, styles and lay-outs, and suburban estates of private developers moving from stockbroker's Tudor to mid-century brick and glass boxes or concrete habitats suggesting tiny airports. The historian should visit the New Towns and the new shopping precincts and supermarkets in older places. He cannot write about mid-century Britain, and its emergence from that so-distant country of 1914 or 1939, simply by sitting in his study, reading books and looking at a few photographs. Yet without the books and photographs history on the ground is formless and much too impressionistic.

CHAPTER 7

Some Varieties of History

'History' generally means to those who read or write it political history: the public history of a country or a continent or the world, the main political events, wars, treaties, legislation, 'progress'; sometimes part of this is narrowed down to diplomatic history. Nowadays 'history' will also include a good deal of economic history, though this has developed almost as a discipline on its own, with its own problems and language and its own initiates. Social history is also admissible, provided awkward questions are not asked about it: is it simply history with the politics left out, or the history of 'everyday things', manners, fashions, houses, schools, 'the people', or is it something much more rigorous and still gradually evolving, the history of class and of social structure? And beyond this one can go on multiplying: the history of art, the history of ideas, ecclesiastical history, military history, constitutional history, imperial and colonial history, agricultural history, urban history, population history (demography), and so on. Each has its own methods and its own experts. Their sources should be apparent in their works, if they contain proper references.

Here we can only look at a few varieties of history which raise particular questions about sources.

I. ECONOMIC HISTORY

One difficulty about economic history for the layman is its growing use of statistics, tables, charts, graphs and mathematical formulae, as well as its evolution of a private language (e.g. block-recursive structures). To the general historian who is only concerned with the findings of investigations this need not matter very much, for the conclusions of an article are usually presented in an intelligible opening or closing paragraph. If, however, one asks for the sources of the data used in the computations presented, one may be in for a rather lengthy enquiry, and may just as well resolve to accept the data as 'given'.

One example must suffice. An article in the *Economic History Review* for April 1968 (criticising and summarising earlier articles on the same subject) on 'Growth in the Inter-War Period: Some more Arithmetic',[1] concluded that economic growth in Britain was as rapid in the twenties as in the thirties and was respectable, in spite of the dip in the rising curve between 1929 and 1933, at a rate of about 2·2 per cent per annum of total output; other indicators, of the growth of employment and the growth of total capital stock, were somewhat smaller. This rate of growth included several of the older industries, and also agriculture, as well as the new industries. Moreover, the rate of growth in this period was shown to be 'as rapid as any of comparable length in British measured history (post-1856)', and better than that of the pre-1914 decade.[2]

Such conclusions, contradicting earlier impressions of the twenties as a time of economic stagnation, and of the thirties as dominated by depression (though historians had already stressed the rapidity of recovery outside the depressed areas, and the importance of the growth of new industries and of the service industries),[3] naturally lead one to ask for the evidence on which the encouraging tables are based. The note on Statistical Sources refers one, for output, to two articles by K. S. Lomax and C. H. Feinstein. The latter gives figures for output and gross domestic product for 1920 to 1962; its Statistical Appendix carries one a little further, citing Lomax's article, and estimates of agricultural output published annually in the government's *Agricultural Statistics*, and referring one to another official publication, the

[1] J. A. Dowie, 'Growth in the Inter-war Period: Some More Arithmetic', *Econ. Hist. Rev.*, XXI, 93–112 (April 1968).

[2] *Ibid.*, 94; cf. 93, 97.

[3] H. W. Richardson, 'The Basis of Economic Recovery in the Nineteen-Thirties', *Econ. Hist. Rev.*, XV, 344–63 (December 1962); *id.*, *Economic Recovery in Britain 1932–39* (London, 1967); C. L. Mowat, *Britain between the Wars* (London, 1955), 432–61.

Central Statistical Office's *National Income Statistics: Sources and Methods* (London, 1956).[1] This last, the first of a series, aims to explain how the government arrived at the estimates of national income and expenditure published annually since 1941 (since 1952 in a White Paper giving summary statistics and in the National Income 'Blue Book').[2] The relevant chapter on Sources mentions tax assessments as the major source for income, statistics of the Ministry of Agriculture and of Customs and Excise for consumers' expenditure, government accounts (including local government and the public corporations) and the Census of Production for capital expenditure and output.[3] The Census of Production has been taken annually since 1948; previously it was conducted in 1907, 1912, 1924, 1930, 1935, and there were partial enquiries under the Import Duties Act in 1933, 1934, and 1937. Lomax's article also used the Census of Production and other government sources for the construction of its series of annual index numbers, supplementing these with 'published information in books, periodicals, academic and trade journals, reports of trade associations, etc.' and with unpublished information from private firms and trade associations.[4]

The construction of tables of production, employment and capital-formation, carried back over half a century or a century, is of course only an aspect of the quantification which much economic history seeks and has always sought. Economic history, we have been told, 'is sweeping all before it'[5]—itself a rather sweeping remark. The term refers to a group of American economic

[1] C. H. Feinstein, 'Production and Productivity 1920-1962', *London and Cambridge Bulletin*, No. 48 (*The Times Review of Industry and Technology*, December 1963), xii–xiv.

[2] E.g., *National Income and Expenditure, 1955*, giving statistics for 1938 and 1946–54.

[3] Central Statistical Office, *National Income Statistics: Sources and Methods* (London, 1956), Ch. III.

[4] K. S. Lomax, 'Production and Productivity Movements in the United Kingdom since 1900', *Journal of the Royal Statistical Society*, series A, 122: 185–210 (1959), especially 191, 194.

[5] Keith Thomas, 'The Tools and the Job' in the series 'New Ways in History', *Times Literary Supplement*, 7 April 1966.

historians, and particularly to R. W. Fogel's *Railroads and American Economic Growth* (Cornell, 1964) which, among other techniques, employs the 'counterfactual conditional concept' of assessing how things might have been if what happened had not happened. This concept, which at first sight arouses distrust, is in fact no more than what historians often do, and will always do until they forswear the use of the word 'if'; it is, of course, used by Fogel in a very refined way. The 'new' economic history—'economic history written by economists' it has been called[1]—can teach historians much provided it makes clear the sources on which it is based and presents its argument and conclusions in straightforward terms.

2. OFFICIAL HISTORY

Official history, that is, historical works sponsored by the government and published under its auspices, has been a phenomenon of the two wars of the century. For the First World War the official military history was written by a soldier, Brigadier-General Sir James Edmonds, for whom it became a life-work; he was still labouring at the final volume when he died in 1956. Recently his work has been criticised on an important point, the comparative statistics of casualties sustained by the Germans and by Britain and France. He produced statistics which supported the 'Westerners" contention that the Germans suffered heavier losses than the Allies at the Somme in 1916, thus giving some justification for the battle; and of his overall statistics, magnifying German losses and paring down the Allies', it has been said that 'his methods of reckoning have been shown to be completely unreliable'.[2] The only official history of any part of the civilian side

[1] G. R. Hawke, 'Mr. Hunt's Study of the Fogel Thesis: A Comment', *History*, 53: 23 (February 1968); this and E. H. Hunt, 'The New Economic History: Professor Fogel's Study of American Railways', *ibid.*, 3–18, are the best introduction to the subject. Cf. M. Desai, 'Some Issues in Econometric History', *Econ. Hist. Rev.*, XXI, 1–16 (1968).

[2] Brian Bond, 'The First World War', in *New Cambridge Modern History*, Vol. XII, 2nd edition, ed., C. L. Mowat (Cambridge, 1968), 197–8, citing articles by M. J. Williams in the *Royal Services Institute Journal* for February 1964 and February 1966.

of the war was the *History of the Ministry of Munitions*, printed in eleven volumes. It was never published, but copies were deposited in the British Museum and a number of other leading libraries, where it can be freely consulted.[1] There was, however, a notable series of the economic and social history of the war published by the Carnegie Endowment for International Peace. These were mostly written by regular or temporary civil servants who had been directly involved in the services they described.[2]

In the Second World War official histories covered both the military and the civilian sides (there was also a medical series). The authors of the military series were either soldiers or historians; those of the civilian series were historians. To understand the character of the civilian series it is essential to read the preface to the first volume, W. K. Hancock and M. M. Gowing, *British War Economy*. Here it is explained that the authors were all historians, chosen in 1942 and acting as a team, though the majority worked in the departments where their main materials were to be found. There was an editorial plan for the whole series, and the editor (Sir Keith Hancock) was responsible to an official committee and to an advisory committee of 'eminent British historians'. The books were originally written not for publication but for 'confidential print', the object being 'to fund experience for government use'. Hence they were expected to be critical, and not just success stories. When it was decided to publish there were some changes in the drafts, especially as to length. In any case the historians 'respected the conventions of government . . . the

[1] D. Hay described it in *Econ. Hist. Rev.*, XIV (1944).

[2] The economic and social history of the First World War in Britain was covered by twenty-four volumes published by the Carnegie Endowment for International Peace as part of a larger series on the 'Economic and Social History of the World War'. There were, to name only a few, volumes by A. L. Bowley on *Prices and Wages in the United Kingdom 1914-1920*, J. A. Salter on *Allied Shipping Control*, H. D. Henderson on *The Cotton Control Board*, T. H. Middleton on *Food Production in War*, R. A. S. Redmayne on the coalmining industry, G. D. H. Cole on *Trade Unionism and Munitions*, *Workshop Control*, and *Labour in the Coal-Mining Industry*, Humbert Wolfe on *Labour Supply and Regulation*, E. M. H. Lloyd on *Experiments in State Control*, C. E. Fayle on shipping, J. C. Stamp on taxation, and W. H. Beveridge on *British Food Control*.

impersonality of the civil service and the collective responsibility
of the Cabinet'. But in the volumes 'devoted to problems of
national economy and administration, there is very little information that cannot be frankly and fully divulged'.[1]

What are the limitations of these official histories as sources or
historical accounts? They cannot give references to any papers in
the official archives, which were closed at the time of writing;
they cannot name names. A sort of denatured history results. 'It
remains an official history—exciting clashes of personality are
most discreetly veiled and the strong tides of the battle for raw
material supplies ebb away in the sands of careful analysis',[2] wrote
one reviewer. Another suspected that the authors would be
tempted to accept the judgment of civil servants because they were
so familiar with their views.[3] The volumes all claim that the
authors were given complete freedom of access to documents; but
clearly the authors would have written differently if not kept
under wraps. None the less, the works can contain frank judgments which may offend some of the actors and overlords: the

[1] W. K. Hancock and M. M. Gowing, *British War Economy* (London, 1949),
ix–xii. This is one of three introductory volumes to the 'History of the Second
World War: United Kingdom Civil Series', the others being M. M. Postan,
British War Production, and R. M. Titmuss, *Problems of Social Policy*. Various
volumes covered Agriculture (K. A. H. Murray), Civil Defence (T. H. O'Brien),
Coal (W. H. B. Court), Economic Blockade (W. N. Medlicott), Financial
Policy (R. S. Sayers), Food (R. J. Hammond), Inland Transport (C. I. Savage),
Manpower (H. M. D. Parker), Merchant Shipping (C. B. A. Behrens), Con-
tracts (W. Ashworth), Raw Materials (J. Hurstfield), Labour in Munition
Factories (P. Inman), and North American Supply (H. Duncan Hall). The
Medical Series described the army, navy and air force's medical history and
also the emergency and civilian medical services: the latter were edited, in two
volumes apiece, by C. L. Dunn and Sir Arthur MacNalty respectively.

The Military Series, edited by J. R. M. Butler, included six volumes by
various hands on Grand Strategy, accounts of various campaigns, *The War at
Sea* by Captain S. W. Roskill and the important four volumes on *The Strategic
Air Offensive* by Sir Charles Webster and A. N. Frankland, *The Defence of the
United Kingdom* by Basil Collier, and three volumes on military government in
various war zones.

[2] J. P. T. Bury in *English Historical Review*, 69: 509 (1954).
[3] W. O. Henderson in *History*, 39: 290–2 (1954).

criticism of the bomber policy in *The Strategic Air Offensive* by Sir Charles Webster and A. N. Frankland is a case in point.[1]

A rather special storm blew up after the publication of M. R. D. Foot's *S.O.E. in France: an Account of the Work of the British Special Operations Executive in France, 1940–1944* (London, 1966). This was an official history written by a very able historian. But it was apparently not based on the full files of the S.O.E., some of which were missing, and though it was vetted by a number of people, it was not submitted to any of the special agents who had worked, at peril of their lives, in France during the war; even stranger, Mr Foot was not allowed to see any of these 'interested parties'[2]. The matter got beyond sarcastic reviews and letters to *The Times*; questions were asked in Parliament. All one can say is that it was something to have an official history of a secret branch at all, and that some of the 'interested parties' had already published their personal histories of the service.[3]

4. THE HISTORY OF SCIENCE

Contemporary historians can be chided for neglecting the history of science. Science is transforming, or is likely to transform, our lives to an extent utterly beyond the experience of any previous generations; ninety per cent of all the scientists in the world's history are living today. The indictment is familiar, but the proper response to it is not clear. Certainly most historians know little or nothing of the history of science; but what *is* the history of science? It can be the history of a series of discoveries, in the laboratories, by research and experiment and, even more, by intuition, imagination, inspiration, discoveries by which the secrets of nature are revealed. All science is historical in the sense that any discovery rests on the previous work of others; research in the literature of the subject must precede the work in the

[1] These volumes contains footnote references to reports, memoranda and committee papers, but do not give the location of the files.

[2] *The Times*, 28 April 1966 (editorial and review).

[3] Jean Overton Fuller, *Double Webs* (London, 1958); Elizabeth Nicholas, *Death Be Not Proud* (London, 1958).

laboratory. The report of some new finding summarises the previous history of the subject. Beyond this, histories of science, of chemistry or physics, biology or engineering, can be written, for scientist or non-scientist; sometimes, as in J. D. Watson's *Double Helix* (London, 1968), the account of the discovery of the chemical structure of DNA, the history of science can be a popular best-seller.[1]

The trouble is that none of this is history: it is much closer to annals. It is the record of events or processes in isolation; to be part of history it must be related to the world outside, it must have roots in the society of the time. Yet to say this is dangerously near saying that the history of science must be the history of inventions, applications, technology: 'science in the service of mankind', a branch of the history of progress. This is much too narrow a view of science, and is likely to produce trivial history—a series of happy accidents occurring in a vacuum. The history of science is at constant risk of either being so technical that the layman cannot follow it, or so plain that the layman scorns it for its banality and feels himself superior to the scientists, of whose work he has been given no clear understanding. In either case he is told chiefly what happened, and little or nothing about why or how it happened, whether it be the history of space exploration or the development of computers.

One way in which science is related to society and becomes part of history is by the decisions about it. Scientific discoveries do not just happen; there were decisions, even decisions of high policy, that led to this subject being investigated, that subject ignored or shelved. The context of the times is important: developments in

[1] There are, of course, plenty of histories of science and of sciences, some more popular than others. K. J. Ridler, *History of Science and Technology* (Library Association Special Subject List No. 48, 1967) is a useful short bibliography. To write the very recent history of various advances in science one would need to consult the chief general science journals: *Nature* (weekly); *Discovery* (monthly: ceased 1966); *Scientific American* (monthly); *New Scientist* (weekly, 1956–   ); *The Advancement of Science* (monthly); *Science Progress* (quarterly). Encyclopedias and their annual supplements are useful for this purpose; also the *Annual Register*, and the notices of scientists in the supplements to the *Dictionary of National Biography*.

society as a whole and in other sciences in particular. The history of science, to be truly historical, must include the history of science policy, of decision-making about science, though it should not consist of this alone. But the history of science policy is little known by most scientists themselves.

Perhaps this is because there is no policy. It is true that much, perhaps most research in universities depends on the training, inclinations or whims of individual scientists, limited only by their capacity and the equipment they can obtain. Business firms may influence the direction of research by the grants they are willing to make to universities for work along particular lines; but these grants are usually sought. The initiative does not come from the companies, which have their own laboratories and research staff, directed towards the commercial activities of the firm. There are, however, the government research councils, notably the Science Research Council (formerly the Department of Scientific and Industrial Research), which by grants and studentships can greatly influence the direction of research. How does the Science Research Council reach its decisions?[1]

What breaks the barrier of silence—or of secrecy or, much more, of ignorance—is war and the fear of war. War uses science and war stimulates research along certain lines; the results may be devastatingly clear. At some point decisions were taken, by people who, with some trouble, may be identified; certainly at some stage politicians were involved in decisions, though these may remain buried in files covered by the Official Secrets Act. None the less, a good deal can be found out, and there are some notable examples.

[1] There is at least one important book on science policy: J. D. Bernal, *The Social Function of Science* (London, 1939; 2nd edition, 1960). A short-lived attempt to bring science to bear on questions of colonial development and national economic policy is described, with the benefit of Cabinet records, in R. M. MacLeod and E. K. Andrews, 'The Committee for Civil Research: Scientific Advice for Economic Development 1925–30', *Minerva*, VII, 680–705 (1969). The authors were members of the Science Policy Research Unit of the University of Sussex. Cf. Eric Hutchinson, 'Scientists and Civil Servants: the struggle over the National Physical Laboratory', *ibid.*, 373–98.

One is the story of the radar system of giving warning of approaching aeroplanes, developed just before the war, in 1935-8. The chain of events and decisions which led to radar as a practical defence system, installed in the nick of time, seems to have been started by H. E. Wimperis, of the Department of Scientific and Industrial Research, lunching at the Athenaeum in October 1934 with A. V. Hill, the physiologist who had been connected with anti-aircraft work in the First World War. Wimperis asked Hill if there was a death ray (radiant energy) which could be used for anti-aircraft defence. Other conversations with various people followed, and in November Wimperis wrote to Lord Londonderry, the Air Secretary, about the possibilities of energy transmission by radiation and its application to air defence, and proposed the appointment of a small committee of 'two or three scientific men' to survey the subject. He suggested Sir Henry Tizard as chairman, Hill, and P. M. S. Blackett, the physicist, and these men were appointed in December, forming, with Wimperis and A. P. Rowe, Wimperis' assistant, as secretary, the Committee for the Scientific Survey of Air Defence.

Meanwhile, Wimperis had consulted Robert Watson-Watt, Superintendent of the Radio Research Laboratory at Slough, about the death ray. A. F. Wilkins, Watson-Watt's assistant, reported that the death ray was not feasible, and was then asked to find what power was needed to produce a detectable signal from an aircraft at a given range. Wilkins found that a plane might be located by the use of radio waves. This was reported to the first meeting of the Tizard Committee. The Committee had no authority, no staff, no facilities; much of its work—confidential interviews in Tizard's flat, secretarial work at his expense—was done privately, and included at least one other lunch at the Athenaeum. The Committee decided on an investigation at a cost of £10,000, and Wimperis got the money; a test was made with a plane flying through the beams of the Daventry radio transmitter, experiments were made at an R.A.F. station at Orfordness and at Bawdsey Manor, and in December 1935 the Treasury approved the building of five radar stations along the southern and eastern coasts. Further vital work was done by Tizard at the Biggin Hill R.A.F. station, persuading the pilots to use the system and practice interceptions with its aid.

There was at the time a parallel movement, which came into association and conflict with Tizard's. This was the work of Winston Churchill and his friend and confidant F. A. Lindemann, 'the Prof', later Lord Cherwell, who was also a physicist. Lindemann had written a letter to *The Times* in August 1934 on 'Science and Air Bombing', and had been lobbying for the appointment of a committee for the scientific investigation of defence. When he and Churchill learned of the existence of the Tizard Committee, Churchill put pressure on MacDonald, the Prime Minister, and Lindemann was added to the Committee. There he pushed his own ideas for night bombing and infra-red detection of planes, and caused so much disagreement—to which Watson-Watt added by pressing for a separate radar development organisation —that after two stormy meetings in June and July 1936 the three original members decided to resign. Instead, the committee was reconstituted, without Lindemann. During the war, of course, Lindemann had the advantage when Churchill became Prime Minister and he served as his scientific adviser.[1]

What are the sources for this important piece of history? We know more of it than of other pieces of the history of science because of the contrast—to many, the duel—between Tizard and Lindemann, two men sharply opposed in character and methods. Lindemann's life was written by Roy Harrod, economist and historian, his Christ Church colleague, and by Lord Birkenhead,[2] Tizard's by R. W. Clark, a writer specialising in the history of recent science and scientists. Clark based his work on Tizard's and Lindemann's papers, which are evidently quite voluminous, on information gained in letters and interviews from many of their surviving colleagues, and from the books written by some of

[1] R. W. Clark, *Tizard* (London, 1965), 105–63, is the source of this account.
[2] Roy Harrod, *The Prof* (London, 1959); Lord Birkenhead, *Prof in Two Worlds* (London, 1961).

them, Rowe and Watson-Watt for example.[1] Whether future historians of science will find better sources—for instance, in the records of the Air Ministry—remains to be seen.

Lindemann, a difficult man in personal relations, and prominent among those supporting the tactic of heavy bombing of Germany later in the war, has been an easy target. During the war he was in charge of the Prime Minister's Statistical Section, a group of some twenty people charged with giving Churchill quantitative information, not necessarily on scientific matters, and reducing long technical briefs to comprehensible ten-line minutes. Not unnaturally the section, with its omniscience and its roving commission, became as unpopular with ministers and officials as Lloyd George's 'Garden Suburb', which served a similar purpose, had been in the other war. A. V. Hill, by then M.P. for Cambridge University, wrote a memorandum in 1940 'on the making of technical decisions by H.M. Government', complaining of the influence of Lindemann who was, he said, 'completely out of touch with his scientific colleagues . . . he has no special knowledge of many of the matters in which he takes a hand'.[2] Professor R. V. Jones, a colleague of Tizard and Lindemann, wrote of both in 'Scientists at War' in *The Times*, 6, 7 and 8 April 1961; C. P. Snow's lectures on *Science and Government* (Oxford, 1961) took up the tale. Both writers were concerned with the relations between science and government and with the question of how to make sure that the government's decisions on science policy are based on sound scientific advice.[3]

Tizard also played a part in what many people would regard as the most important decision ever made on policy about science, the decision to manufacture the atomic bomb. Acting for the Committee of Imperial Defence he obtained and distributed small supplies of uranium, giving some to Professor M. L. Oliphant of

[1] A. P. Rowe, *One Story of Radar* (Cambridge, 1948); Sir R. Watson-Watt, *Three Steps to Victory* (London, 1958).

[2] R. W. Clark, *Tizard*, 244.

[3] R. V. Jones, 'Scientists and Statesmen: the example of Henry Tizard', *Minerva*, IV, 202–14 (1966).

Birmingham to help with the work of two German refugees, O. R. Frisch and R. E. Peierls, who were following up the splitting of an uranium atom by Otto Hahn and Lise Meitner (Frisch's aunt) in December 1938. Frisch's and Peierls' memorandum 'on the construction of a "super-bomb" based on a nuclear chain reaction in uranium' was sent to Tizard in March 1940; his committee formed another committee to go into the matter, the 'Maud' committee. This committee reported in July 1941 that the use of uranium for making a bomb and for manufacturing power was feasible.

Of the decisions which followed we have a very full account. The report was considered by the government's Science Advisory Committee, consisting of scientists of great eminence, Appleton, Hill, Sir Henry Dale, Sir Edward Mellanby, A. C. Egerton, under the chairmanship of Lord Hankey, the former secretary of the Cabinet. They decided, after cross-examining the members of the Maud Committee and other experts, that Britain should go ahead with the project of making an atomic bomb, but that the necessary plant should be constructed in Canada or the United States. The decision about the plant was not lightly reached and there was opinion within the government, notably that of Lindemann, that the plant should be in Britain or, in the last resort, in Canada. The decision was made on technical grounds: the size of the plant and the slow rate of the production process meant that the plant could not be located where there was danger of air attack.[1] Meanwhile, two Americans, Dr Vannevar Bush and Dr J. B. Conant of the Office of Scientific Research and Development, had been told of the work of the Maud Committee and were quickly given its reports. At this time American work on nuclear fission was behind Britain's, and the Americans, convinced by the Maud reports of the feasibility of an atomic bomb, invited British co-operation. The British government stalled, sceptical of the necessary secrecy being maintained.[2] As a result, the Americans went ahead on their

[1] Margaret Gowing, *Britain and Atomic Energy 1939-1945* (London, 1964), 93–103.
[2] *Ibid.*, 94, 117–24.

own, and soon outstripped the British, whom they then barred out; and though the work on the bomb did finally engage several British scientists in the United States, it remained essentially an American achievement.[1]

We know all this, with dates, names, places, because of an official history, that of Mrs Margaret Gowing, the historian and archivist of the United Kingdom Atomic Energy Authority, which commissioned her to write *Britain and Atomic Energy 1939–1945* and gave her full access to all the papers. 'In two cases only,' she writes, 'have I omitted quotations of documents because it was clear that they could harm the public interest.' All that is lacking is references to the documents, and these, 'A Note on Documentation' promises, 'will be available in confidential print and will be accessible to scholars when the documents concerned are publicly available'. Certainly the official nature of the work has not prevented fullness of detail and the utmost frankness; for the latter, see the account of Churchill's interview with the great Danish physicist, Niels Bohr, on 16 May 1944. Bohr wanted desperately to put to Churchill the danger of letting the use of the bomb, whose production was by then assured, rest in the hands of a single country. Churchill, concerned only with Anglo-American relations, and having already sold the pass in the one-sided Quebec agreement on the future development of atomic power, simply would not see the point and was almost rude in his dismissal of Bohr.[2]

By contrast, we know almost nothing of another all-important decision, that taken secretly by the Attlee government to go ahead, in view of the continuing refusal of the Americans to share their 'secrets', with the independent development of an atomic bomb by Great Britain. Attlee's memoirs, and Francis Williams' *A Prime Minister Remembers*, are singularly uncommunicative on the subject. Fortunately, Mrs Gowing's second volume can be expected to set the record straight. Into other fields of science, not covered by official histories, it looks as if history may never

[1] Margaret Gowing, *Britain and Atomic Energy 1939–1945* (London, 1964), xiv.
[2] *Ibid.*, 352–5.

venture. Articles in the journals, stray reminiscences and memoirs, obituaries, the work of a few popular writers with an interest in scientific subjects, the occasional history of a science-based company—these will constitute the historical literature of a vast field of human endeavour. Sources for anything more will not exist, for records will not have been made, or if made, preserved.

CHAPTER 8

The Zinoviev Letter: A Case Study

It may be interesting to study a particular episode in the history of this period, to see how evidence about it accumulates by degrees, without necessarily clearing up all points of obscurity or debate. The Zinoviev Letter, purportedly signed by Zinoviev and two other members of the Executive Committee of the Communist International and dated 15 September 1924, was addressed to the Communist Party in Britain. It was written at the time when the first Labour government was in office and was unpopular because of two commercial treaties with Soviet Russia signed the previous August. The Letter, though urging pressure for the ratification of the treaties, was hostile to the Labour government and upbraided the Communist Party for weakness in its agitation among soldiers and sailors: cells should be established in all units of the troops, and in munition works.

The text of the Letter was published in the press on Saturday, 25 October, four days before polling in the general election on Wednesday, 29 October. It followed a frenzied campaign against Labour at a time when 'Bolshevism' was still a scare word, and it could be read as showing how villainous the Russians were and therefore how untrustworthy was Labour, who had signed the treaties with Russia. Moreover, the Letter appeared to be authentic since it was accompanied by the text of an official protest from the Foreign Office to Rakovsky, the Russian *chargé d'affaires* in London. 'We're bunkered' (so quoted, but probably bowdlerised) said J. H. Thomas, on seeing the Letter; and it may have contributed to Labour's defeat in the election though, in fact, the Liberals were the heaviest losers. Certainly its publication was well-timed to help the Conservatives to victory, and the confusion it caused in Labour ranks was not relieved by any explanation or rebuttal from MacDonald, the Prime Minister and Foreign

Secretary, until he spoke at Cardiff on Monday evening, the 27th, and again on Tuesday on the eve of the poll. Only the Labour *Daily Herald* called it a forgery.

The main questions about the Letter are: (1) was it forged, and by whom, (2) how did it reach London, (3) how many copies were circulating, and did they come from a single source (the original was never seen by anyone known to the historical record), (4) was MacDonald obtuse in his handling of the Letter, or was he stalling to prevent its publication before the election, (5) why was it published when it was, and (6) how culpable was the Foreign Office in publishing it without MacDonald's authorisation.

All that was known at the time was the text of the Letter and the accompanying protest,[1] and also that the *Daily Mail* had had a copy of its own. Rakovsky, on the 25th, issued a statement denouncing the Letter as a 'gross forgery' and protesting against its publication without his having been notified first; he also pointed out that the titles of the signatories were incorrect: there had never been earlier Communist Internationals. MacDonald's explanation on the Monday was that the Foreign Office had received the Letter on 10 October and had sent it on to him on the 15th but, because of his election tour, he had not received it till the 16th. He sent it back with a minute that great care must be taken to ensure its authenticity; if it was authentic it must be published at once, and to save time a letter of protest should be drafted. He received the draft letter of protest on the 23rd, and sent it back with alterations, but uninitialled, expecting to get it back again, with proofs of the Zinoviev Letter's authenticity, before publication. Instead, Letter and protest were published in the morning papers on Saturday the 25th over the signature of J. D. Gregory, head of the Northern department of the Foreign Office. However, MacDonald went on to exonerate the civil servants from any blame: they had acted hastily, knowing his hatred of propaganda. He expressed his own doubts on the question of authenticity. His speech on Tuesday the 28th added the point that he had heard that the Letter was being discussed in a London club four days before

[1] See Appendix.

the Foreign Office had received it (Foreign Office officials, Gregory and William Strang, had come down to Wales to explain matters to him over the week-end).[1] The Labour Cabinet appointed a committee to investigate the Letter's authenticity, but had no time to reach a conclusion before it fell.[2] The new Conservative government was less cautious: Austen Chamberlain, the Foreign Secretary, wrote to Rakovsky on 21 November that the government had 'no doubt whatsoever' about authenticity.[3]

So far, information had come only from the press, but when Parliament met questions were raised there. In the debate on the address from the throne at the opening of the new Parliament, MacDonald raised the question how a newspaper had got an identical copy of the Letter days or weeks before the Foreign Office (in fact, this was not so). J. R. Clynes asked about the new Cabinet's sub-committee which had gone into the Letter's authenticity, only to be told by Sir William Joynson-Hicks, the Home Secretary, that the Cabinet accepted fully the word of the members 'as men of business' (they were simply fellow-Cabinet members) that it was authentic. Later, Austen Chamberlain, the Foreign Secretary, made three points: publication by the Foreign Office was due to a misunderstanding between the Office and MacDonald; the Foreign Office was satisfied of the Letter's authenticity but could not divulge its reasons: 'it is of the essence of a Secret Service that it must be secret'; and the Foreign Office had four separate copies of the Letter, each received independently of the others (this statement has never been subjected to any examination or explanation). MacDonald's reply again raised the question of a newspaper's getting a copy of the Letter at the same

[1] L. Chester, S. Fay and H. Young, *The Zinoviev Letter* (London, 1967), 13, 116–17.

[2] *Ibid.*, 140–3 describes the discussion in the Labour Cabinet about an enquiry on 31 October 1924. No source for this is given; it is clearly Tom Jones' diary, which was published two years later (*Whitehall Diary*, I [Oxford, 1969], 299–301).

[3] For the whole affair, see L. Chester *et al.*, or earlier accounts in my *Britain between the Wars*, 188–94, and R. W. Lyman, *The First Labour Government* (London, 1957), 257–61, 286–8.

time as the Foreign Office; of the Letter he said that to him its authenticity was not proved, and he asked for a proper enquiry. On the fact that only copies of the Letter existed, Chamberlain asserted that the original had been received and destroyed by the British Communists (no proof of this has ever been offered).[1]

J. H. Thomas, speaking in the same debate, after Chamberlain, elaborated the point that the Letter's publication was no surprise to the Conservatives in their election campaign. He quoted *The Times* of 27 October as saying that for the past week 'it was a matter of common gossip that a message from Zinoviev had been intercepted, and on Friday the [24th] it was known that the text would be published the following morning'. It added that it was pressing for its publication 'for at least a fortnight'. Thomas also quoted the *Manchester Evening Chronicle* of 22 October, reporting from London 'that before polling day comes a bombshell will burst and it will be connected with Zinoviev'.[2]

In the next few months there were various denials of the Letter's authenticity, but little or no attention was paid to them. Zinoviev's denial was published in the *Communist Review* in December 1924. A delegation of the T.U.C., which was in Moscow, investigated the Comintern's files in November and December, and could find no trace of the Letter: this report was published in 1929.[3] Mrs M. A. Hamilton's life of MacDonald, published in 1925, showed up inconsistencies in the text of the protest note to argue that MacDonald had expected to receive it back before publication.[4] In April 1927 a book entitled *Anglo-Soviet Forgeries* was published in England which discussed the Zinoviev Letter among other forgeries. That summer one of the forgers described in the book, Druzhelovsky, on trial in Moscow, gave evidence about the fabrication of the Letter in Berlin, mentioning two men whom we now know to have been

[1] 179 *H.C. Deb.* 5 s., 67–9, 197, 310–11, 672–4, 688–90 (9, 10, 15 December 1924).

[2] *Ibid.*, 741–5 (15 December 1924).

[3] T.U.C. General Council, *The Zinoviev Letter: Report of Investigation by the British Delegation to Russia* (London, 1925).

[4] See below, pp. 210–12.

connected with the forgery, Bellegarde and Gumansky, and also Paciorkowski, a Polish captain 'connected with other Intelligence Services'. Following the Commons debate in March 1928, Chicherin, the Commissar for Foreign Affairs, issued a press statement pointing out the evidence obtained at this trial. Few people in England were then ready to credit it.[1]

The whole question of the Letter's authenticity, and the circulation of copies of it, was reopened early in 1928 in a court case concerning speculation in French francs: a Mrs Dyne was sued by a firm of bankers, and implicated Gregory, a friend of hers, who was involved in the same speculations. A civil service enquiry was at once held into speculation among Foreign Office staff: Sir Warren Fisher, Permanent Secretary of the Treasury, headed it. MacDonald and Thomas were allowed to give evidence, having been given a statement in 1924 (made originally to the *Daily Herald*) by Violet Digby, a former maid of Mrs Dyne, which suggested collaboration between Mrs Dyne and Gregory at that time, and also that the publication of the Letter had been done by Gregory 'when the Prime Minister's back was turned'. Gregory was dismissed the service after the Fisher enquiry, but the report denied that there had been any plot to publish the Zinoviev Letter.[2] The Labour Party then asked for a debate on the Fisher report, and the government agreed: but before it took place some more partial information was thrown into the arena.

This was contained in a long letter by Thomas Marlowe, editor of the *Daily Mail* in 1924, to the *Observer*. Marlowe stated that he had first heard of the Letter on Thursday, 23 October, from 'an old and trusted friend' who told him that MacDonald knew all about it but was trying to avoid publication. He said it had been circulated that day to the Foreign Office, Home Office, Admiralty and War Office. Marlowe then described how 'telephonic soundings soon put me in touch with another friend' who came to see him but said he did not think he could get a copy of the Letter. 'I insisted that I must have it, and at length he promised that if he

[1] L. Chester *et. al.*, *The Zinoviev Letter*, 46–7, 57.
[2] *Ibid.*, 150–6.

could obtain the approval of a third person he would send me a copy through the post.' Half an hour later another friend called with 'the thing in his pocket', but would not give it to Marlowe without consulting a friend. Next day, Friday afternoon, they met again and Marlowe got his copy, and found the other one in the post on his return to his office. He had the Letter set up in print, and sent proofs and a circular note to other editors, and also phoned up *The Times* to tell it what was on the way. The Foreign Office was informed, and Sir Eyre Crowe, the Permanent Secretary, then decided to publish the Letter rather than permit disclosures by the newspapers: Gregory had nothing to do with the decision, but signed the note of protest as head of the relevant department. The official papers reached some of the newspaper offices a few minutes before Marlowe's proofs. Marlowe added that it was obvious (in fact it is not obvious, and the Fisher report denied it)[1] that official publication was forced by his action; but for this there would have been a delay of days or a week before Rakovsky's reply was received: 'Mr. MacDonald would have succeeded in delaying publication until it could do his party no harm.' Marlowe also told (what was his source?) of the progress of the Letter in the Foreign Office after its arrival there on 10 October. He denied that Gregory was one of his sources of the Letter.[2]

The Commons debate took place on 19 March 1928. Mac-Donald went over the timetable of his handling of the Letter, and made the point that the copies which reached various departments went to the Intelligence Departments of these departments. He asked who Marlowe's friends were, implying that they were members of the Intelligence services: 'it is of the greatest importance to the free public life of this country that we should know who these various gentlemen are and how they came into possession of the document.' Baldwin, replying, began by asserting that Chicherin had heard of the Letter from Rakovsky on 24 October and had questioned Zinoviev, who admitted that the Letter had

[1] *Ibid.*, 111–12.
[2] *Observer*, 4 March 1928.

been sent; Chicherin then decided that they must denounce it as a forgery. He refused to disclose the evidence for this, but offered to let MacDonald see it. He made the cryptic statement that he understood they were to be confronted today with an affidavit from someone who would swear that he had forged the Letter. He went on to charge MacDonald, once again, with intending to delay publication, saying that, if he intended publishing it, his wish being anticipated could be no grievance. He also asserted, though refusing to give his evidence, that the Communist Party had discussed the Letter on 10 October, implying that Marlowe could have heard of it from that source. His trump card was a statement, which he read out, more or less asserting this. The statement had been made only two days before by a gentleman in the City, unconnected with office or politics. His name was Conrad Donald imThurn. ImThurn's statement was that he had met a business friend 'in close touch with Communist circles in this country' on the evening of 8 October; after their business conversation the man had mentioned the arrival of an extraordinary letter from Moscow sent to the British Communist headquarters. ImThurn asked him for the text and was given it at 9.30 next morning. He decided to bring it to the attention of the government departments concerned and to get it published as soon as his informant could settle his affairs and get to a place of safety. When this had been done he gave it to a 'trusted City friend' who was in close touch with the *Daily Mail*. He had no official sources of information, and was from first to last solely responsible for obtaining the text and securing its publication in the *Daily Mail*. His motives were solely patriotic.

There were further speeches by James Maxton, Saklatvala, the Communist M.P., and the Attorney General, but the only one of importance was the closing speech by J. H. Thomas. He read the whole of Violet Digby's statement, which the Dyne court case had confirmed in its accuracy, and he questioned the imThurn statement as inconsistent with what was known of the circulation of the Letter in the departments, where it was not taken seriously. He made another new point, that MacDonald could not (as

Conservatives claimed he should have done) speak about the Letter's publication on the day, Saturday the 25th, because he was told that afternoon from London, in reply to his question why it had been published, that he had initialled it. He knew he had not: to say so would be to throw over the civil service. But the government won the ensuing division by 326 votes to 132, and there was no enquiry.[1]

Nor was there any enquiry or even much interest in the press about the mysterious Mr imThurn—who died two years later.[2] The matter simply faded away. Gregory's memoirs, *On the Edge of Diplomacy* (London, 1929), were uninformative. Sir Wyndham Childs, head of the Special Branch at Scotland Yard, in his *Episodes and Reflections* (London, 1930), declared of the Letter 'there was absolutely no reason to think that this particular effusion was genuine'.[3] Subsequent scraps of information could be gleaned from biographies and memoirs years later.[4] Sir Frederick Maurice, in his *Life of Viscount Haldane*, Vol. II (London, 1939), printed letters which Sir Eyre Crowe had sent to Haldane stating that the Foreign Office had received after the election proof that Zinoviev had sent the Letter; publication had been due to his misunderstanding of MacDonald's intentions.[5] Harold Nicolson, in his *King George the Fifth* (London, 1952), printed Crowe's letter to MacDonald written just after publication; the King had added, 'suppose there is *no doubt* that Zinoviev's Letter is *genuine*? I see the Communists say it is a forgery.'[6] Hugh Dalton, in his memoirs (1953), explained Baldwin's cryptic reference to an affidavit from the forger in his speech of 19 March 1928. MacDonald had had, just before the debate, a letter from one Dombrowski from Paris, offering information on the Letter. An emissary was sent to Paris who saw Dombrowski and another Russian: they said they were

[1] 215 *H.C.Deb.* 5 s., 47–110 (19 March 1924).

[2] L. Chester *et al.*, *op. cit.*, 170–1.

[3] *Ibid.*, 93, 116–17, 189.

[4] Brought together in R. W. Lyman, *First Labour Government*, 286–9.

[5] Sir F. Maurice, *Life of Lord Haldane*, II (London, 1939), 172–4, cited in Lyman, *loc. cit.*

[6] Sir Harold Nicolson, *King George the Fifth* (London, 1952), 402.

the forgers and offered to provide proof for twenty pounds. The offer was discussed by MacDonald and several of his colleagues; fearing they might be double-crossed and would appear ludicrous to the government for having bribed two White Russian spies, they decided to do nothing. The same extracts from Dalton's diary give MacDonald's version of why Crowe had been so convinced of the Letter's authenticity: (1) because 'the Secret Service Agent who gave it to the F.O. had received it from a man "who had never been known to make a mistake"' and (2) because a police spy at a Communist Party meeting had heard that an important letter from Zinoviev was on the way. Crowe had not, however, troubled to ring up MacDonald to give him this information.[1] This was confirmed in Beatrice Webb's diary, published in 1956: in the final Cabinet of the Labour government (after the incomplete enquiry launched into the Letter's authenticity) it was stated that the copy of the Letter came 'from the most trusted agent of the F.O. in Moscow on October 10th'.[2] The same year revealed some more information in Lord Strang's *Home and Abroad* (London, 1956).[3]

There was no further light on the Zinoviev Letter until a *Sunday Times* team published the results of their investigations in 1967. This solved some mysteries and enlarged the conspiratorial element, but still left much unexplained. Its sources were interviews with several survivors, a typed copy of a diary of imThurn, and a manuscript account written in 1956 by Major Guy Kindersley, Conservative M.P. for Hitchin for many years from 1923 onwards.

First, as to the forgery. The authors claim that the Zinoviev Letter was forged in Berlin by three Russians, Bellegarde, Gumansky and Friede, using a single sheet of Third International notepaper stolen from the Soviet embassy by Druzhelovsky. The evidence is the testimony of Bellegarde's widow, living in London in 1966; it confirms the information given in the trial of

---

[1] Hugh Dalton, *Call Back Yesterday* (London, 1953), 176–8.
[2] *Beatrice Webb's Diaries 1924–1932*, ed. M. Cole (London, 1956), 49.
[3] See below, pp. 210–11.

Druzhelovsky in 1928.[1] Forging a letter is, however, child's play compared to getting it transmitted and accepted as authentic. This question the authors partially answer by bringing in Paciorkowski, also mentioned in the Druzhelovsky trial though not known to Mme Bellegarde. They do not prove that Paciorkowski, a member of the Polish Intelligence, actually was the agent who transmitted the letter to the British Secret Service, but they do produce indirect evidence of his part. It comes from the diary of Maciej Rataj, Speaker of the Polish House of Deputies in 1923–8; the diary was published in Warsaw in 1965. The entry for 9 November 1924 has Sikorski, the Polish prime minister, claiming that he was the author of the Letter, and that it was manufactured out of instructions from the International in Moscow which the General Staff had received. Gregory 'was helpful in exploiting the forgery'. This entry is supplemented by rough notes in which Sikorski is quoted as saying that the forgery was the work of 'our Deuxième Bureau'. Paciorkowski was a lieutenant-colonel in this Bureau.[2] This, of course, gets us no further as to how the Letter, or a copy, actually reached London, and by whose hands.

The book does, however, tell a lot more about imThurn: it is here that new complexities are introduced into the story, and the mystery of the number of copies of the Letter circulating in London is partially solved. Conrad imThurn was director of a company of émigré Russians using a fleet of former Russian cargo ships. He himself was English, and had been in MI5 during the war. His role, once he had got wind of the Letter's existence from 'X'[3]—he never had a copy—was a self-imposed mission of prying, meddling and bluff carried on for two weeks to force publication of this piece of Bolshevist villainy which he feared the government might otherwise suppress. He pestered his contacts in MI5, Sir Wyndham Childs of the Special Branch of Scotland Yard, and Naval Intelligence, until he was told that 'circulation' of copies to

[1] L. Chester *et al.*, *op. cit.*, 51–7; see above, pp. 202–3.
[2] *Ibid.*, 58–62.
[3] ImThurn's diary, *ibid.*, 197–200. 'X' is not identified; the authors think he may have been Paciorkowski.

departments was taking place (on 22 October). He saw *The Times'* lobby correspondent. And through his friend Kindersley he met Lord Younger, treasurer of the Conservative Party, and Sir Stanley Jackson, the chairman. They decided to see that the Letter was published in *The Times*, and they agreed to guarantee imThurn £7,500 for his informant 'X', whose actions had put him in some danger; imThurn was to raise another £2,500 for the same purpose.[1] The authors infer that the Tory chiefs called in Sir Reginald Hall, ex-Director of Naval Intelligence and more recently Principal Agent of the Conservative Party. As for Marlowe's two copies, the authors argue that Marlowe heard of the Letter from Hall, but got one copy from Lieutenant-Colonel Frederick Browning, another former intelligence man from MI1C, who was given it by Admiral Sinclair, head of MI1C. ImThurn saw Browning on October 23, but the authors do not stress this connection, suggesting that Browning was first alerted by Hall. Marlowe's second copy, they think, must have come from an anonymous civil servant in the Home Office or from someone else. One story links Marlowe and Sinclair, the two dining together at the Savoy on October 24 (Friday). But Marlowe had his two copies by that afternoon.[2]

ImThurn's reappearance (or in public his first appearance) on the scene in 1928 was not quite as accidental as Baldwin's speech implied. The coming debate might put the Conservatives in a difficulty, after the doubts about Gregory's conduct raised in the Dyne case and the Fisher enquiry. Major Kindersley was, not surprisingly, the intermediary; he visited the new Conservative Director of Publicity, Major (later Sir) Joseph Ball, another ex-Intelligence man, and later introduced him to imThurn. Then, on the morning of the debate (19 March), imThurn met Baldwin at a lunch at the house of J. C. C. Davidson, the new party Chairman; the other guests were Kindersley, Ball, and the Attorney General, Sir Douglas Hogg. It was decided that imThurn should prepare a statement for Baldwin to read (it was, as we now know, far from

[1] *Ibid.*, 80, 201–2.
[2] *Ibid.*, 70–109; imThurn's diary, *ibid.*, 197–200.

accurate, to say the least; for one thing, imThurn had never had a copy of the Letter at all).¹ ImThurn, or his informant 'X', had, however, never been paid off, and he now asked for the fulfilment of the guarantee of £7,500. He was paid £5,000 by a cheque drawn in Ball's favour by Davidson, the stub marked 'CDiT'. Ball paid the sum to imThurn, who acknowledged it in letters of 2 April 1928, explaining that 'X' would sail at once as a deck hand for the Argentine, where he would live as an Argentine national, having been supplied with Argentine papers. He would be paid £158 per annum for ten years, and then the remaining £2,500.² Why 'X' had not made his escape in 1924 and now had to make it in 1928 is not explained. The authors think the Argentine story was a blind to impress the Conservatives and cover up imThurn's tracks. The real obligation lay in Poland.³

The authors also contribute something to answering the question why Crowe decided to publish the Letter and protest without MacDonald's authority. Drawing on the memories of Lord Strang, then William Strang, Second Secretary in the Northern Department of the Foreign Office, and other officials, they show that the text of the Zinoviev Letter reached the Foreign Office on 10 October, but was not 'registered' as officially received until the 14th, after routine enquiries over the week-end had decided the Office to treat it seriously. Strang, who was one of the first officials to see it, first wrote a short minute discounting it, but was then told that Crowe attached great importance to it and thought it should be published; he sent it forward with a longer minute, and it reached Gregory, who (on the 14th) minuted that he doubted the wisdom of publication: its authenticity would be at once denied.⁴ It then went on to MacDonald. Crowe had apparently received the Letter from another source (presumably another of the four copies which Austen Chamberlain said the Office had

¹ *Ibid.*, 162–4.
² ImThurn's diary, *ibid.*, 176–80, 204–6.
³ *Ibid.*, 186–8, 203 (postscript of letter of imThurn to Kindersley, March 1928: 'Have just had a cable from Warsaw and have communicated with Ball. They *must* settle up with my friend now and finish.').
⁴ *Ibid.*, 67–9.

had), as Dalton's memoirs and Beatrice Webb's diary had recorded,[1] and the authors suggest that this may have been Captain Sidney Reilly, 'the spy who never made a mistake'.[2] As for the responsibility for publishing the protest (and the Letter), this must rest with Gregory and Crowe. Strang recorded in his autobiography *Home and Abroad* (London, 1956) that when Gregory was signing the protest note he pointed out to him that the draft had not been initialled by MacDonald. Gregory's reply was that he couldn't help that: Crowe had said that the note was to go off. When Strang made the same point to Crowe next morning (Saturday the 25th) in reply to MacDonald's query from Wales about the publication, Crowe replied: 'I hadn't noticed that. I must now wait for the storm to break upon my devoted head.'[3]

But there was, and had always been, other evidence of the Foreign Office's haste to publish besides Crowe's conviction of the Letter's genuineness and Gregory's anti-Soviet bias. The protest note is somewhat repetitious, because it was published as Mac-Donald had sent it back on the 23rd, with new sections written by MacDonald without the parts to be discarded being crossed out. Mrs Mary Agnes Hamilton, MacDonald's biographer who knew him well, pointed this out in her life of him published in 1925, knowing of this curious habit of his when revising drafts.[4]

Since the publication of *The Zinoviev Letter* in 1967 not much more has come to light. Tom Jones' *Whitehall Diary*, I (Oxford, 1969) records the discussion in the Labour Cabinet on 31 October 1924.[5] The papers of J. C. C. Davidson, the Conservative Party Chairman in 1928, published in 1969, add information about the lunch at his house on 19 March, and also relate that Kindersley

[1] See above, p. 207.
[2] L. Chester *et al.*, *op. cit.*, 190–5.
[3] *Ibid.*, 113, quoting Strang's *Home and Abroad*. For more on Crowe's responsibility, *ibid.*, 117–21.
[4] *Ibid.*, 114–15, citing M. A. Hamilton (pseud. 'Iconoclast'), *J. Ramsay MacDonald 1923–1925* (London, 1925).
[5] See above, p. 201, note 2.

proposed in February 1956 to publish his account of the Zinoviev
affair and was dissuaded by Ball and Davidson. The papers are
silent about the payment of £5,000 to imThurn.[1]

Is this the end of the road? We still have no full life of
MacDonald, which may have something to add. To return to the
first question, was it a forgery? One argument in favour of this is
the style of the Zinoviev Letter: it is so pat, containing so much
that anti-Bolshevists would like to pin on the Russians.[2] Professor
Medlicott has recently turned this argument on its head: there
were plenty of genuine Russian documents of the time in this
style. He quotes instructions from the Communist International to
the Communist Party of Great Britain on 10 October 1924,
which were seized in the raid on the offices of Arcos, the Russian
trading agency, in 1927, and published in a White Paper (Cmd.
2682) and also in a collection of Russian documents (Jean Degras,
ed., *The Communist International 1919–1943*: Oxford, 1960).[3] In
fact the argument can go either way; why send instructions on
10 October if they had been sent on 15 September? Sources are
the historian's raw material, deduction and imagination his guides.
They can no more establish the truth about everything in the past
in the twentieth century than in any earlier century. But they can
help us to approach it.

[1] R. R. James, *Memoirs of a Conservative*, 203–4.
[2] I argued this in *Britain between the Wars*, 194.
[3] W. N. Medlicott, *Contemporary England*, 205–6.

Appendix

I. THE ZINOVIEV LETTER

Executive Committee,   Very Secret
   Third Communist International.

                                    To the Central Committee,
                                    British Communist Party.

Presidium,
   September 15th, 1924.
   Moscow.

Dear Comrades,

The time is approaching for the Parliament of England to consider the Treaty concluded between the Governments of Great Britain and the S.S.S.R. for the purpose of ratification. The fierce campaign raised by the British bourgeoisie around the question shows that the majority of the same, together with reactionary circles, are against the Treaty for the purpose of breaking off an agreement consolidating the ties between the proletariats of the two countries leading to the restoration of normal relations between England and the S.S.S.R.

The proletariat of Great Britain, which pronounced its weighty word when danger threatened of a break-off of the past negotiations, and compelled the Government of MacDonald to conclude the Treaty, must show the greatest possible energy in the further struggle for ratification and against the endeavours of British capitalists to compel Parliament to annul it.

It is indispensable to stir up the masses of the British proletariat to bring into movement the army of unemployed proletarians whose position can be improved only after a loan has been granted to the S.S.S.R. for the restoration of the economics and when business collaboration between the British and Russian proletariats has been put in order. It is imperative that the group in the Labour Party sympathising with the Treaty should bring increased pressure to bear upon the Government and Parliamentary circles in favour of the ratification of the Treaty.

Keep close observation over the leaders of the Labour Party, because these may easily be found in the leading strings of the bourgeoisie. The foreign policy of the Labour Party as it is, already represents an inferior copy of the policy of the Curzon Government. Organise a campaign of disclosure of the foreign policy of MacDonald.

The I.K.K.I. (Executive Committee, Third [Communist] International) will willingly place at your disposal the wide material in its possession regarding the activities of British Imperialism in the Middle and Far East. In the meanwhile, however, strain every nerve in the struggle for the ratification of the Treaty, in favour of a continuation of negotiations regarding the regulation of relations between the S.S.S.R. and England. A settlement of relations between the two countries will assist in the revolutionising of the international and British Proletariat not less than a successful rising in any of the working districts of England, as the establishment of close contact between the British and Russian proletariat, the exhcange of delegations and workers, etc., will make it possible for us to extend and develop the propaganda of ideas of Leninism in England and the Colonies. Armed warfare must be preceded by a struggle against the inclinations to compromise which are embedded among the majority of British workmen, against the ideas of evolution and peaceful extermination of capitalism. Only then will it be possible to count upon complete success of an armed insurrection. In Ireland and the Colonies the case is different; there there is a national question, and this represents too great a factor for success for us to waste time on a prolonged preparation of the working class.

But even in England, as other countries, where the workers are politically developed, events themselves may more rapidly revolutionise the working masses than propaganda. For instance, a strike movement, repressions by the Government etc.

From your last report it is evident that agitation-propaganda work in the army is weak, in the navy a very little better. Your explanation that the quality of the members attracted justifies the quantity is right in principle, nevertheless it would be desirable to have cells in all the units of the troops, particularly among those quartered in the large centres of the country, and also among factories working on munitions and at military store depots. We request that the most particular attention be paid to these latter.

In the event of danger of war, with the aid of the latter and in contact with the transport workers, it is possible to paralyse all the military

Appendix

preparations of the bourgeoisie, and make a start in turning an imperialist war into a class war. Now more than ever we should be on our guard. Attempts at intervention in China show that world imperialism is still full of vigour and is once more making endeavours to restore its shaken position and cause a new war, which as its final objective is to bring about the break-up of the Russian Proletariat and the suppression of the budding world revolution, and further would lead to the enslavement of the colonial peoples. 'Danger of War', 'The Bourgeoisie seek War', 'Capital fresh Markets'—these are the slogans which you must familiarise the masses with, with which you must go to work into the mass of the proletariat. These slogans will open to you the doors of comprehension of the masses, will help you to capture them and march under the banner of Communism.

The Military Section of the British Communist Party, so far as we are aware, further suffers from a lack of specialists, the future directors of the British Red Army.

It is time you thought of forming such a group, which together with the leaders, might be in the event of an outbreak of active strife, the brain of the military organisation of the party.

Go attentively through the lists of the military 'cells' detailing from them the more energetic and capable men, turn attention to the more talented military specialists who have for one reason or another, left the Service and hold Socialist views. Attract them into the ranks of the Communist Party if they desire honestly to serve the proletariat and desire in the future to direct not the blind mechanical forces in the service of the bourgeoisie, but a national army.

Form a directing operative head of the Military Section.

Do not put this off to a future moment, which may be pregnant with events and catch you unprepared.

Desiring you all success, both in organisation and in your struggle.

With Communist Greetings,

President of the Presidium of the I.K.K.I.

Member of the Presidium: McMANUS.
Secretary: KUUSINEN.

2. THE LETTER OF PROTEST

Mr. MacDonald to M. Rakovsky[1]

Foreign Office, October 24, 1924.

Sir,

I have the honour to invite your attention to the enclosed copy of a letter which has been received by the Central Committee of the British Communist Party from the Presidium of the Executive Committee of the Communist International, over the signature of M. Zinoviev, its president, dated the 15th September. The letter contains instructions to British subjects to work for the violent overthrow of existing institutions in this country, and for the subversion of His Majesty's armed forces as a means to that end.

2. It is my duty to inform you that His Majesty's Government cannot allow this propaganda and must regard it as a direct intervention from outside in British domestic affairs.

3. No one who understands the constitution and the relationships of the Communist International will doubt its intimate connection and contact with the Soviet Government. No Government will ever tolerate an arrangement with a foreign Government by which the latter is in formal diplomatic relations of the correct kind with it, whilst at the same time a propagandist body organically connected with that foreign Government encourages and even orders subjects of the former to plot and plan revolutions for its overthrow. Such conduct is not only a grave departure from the rules of international comity, but a violation of specific and solemn undertakings repeatedly given to His Majesty's Government.

4. So recently as the 4th June of last year the Soviet Government made the following solemn agreement with His Majesty's Government:

'The Soviet Government undertakes not to support with funds or in any other form persons or bodies or agencies or institutions whose aim is to spread discontent or to foment rebellion in any part of the British Empire . . . and to impress upon its officers and officials the full and continuous observance of these conditions.'

[1] *Parliamentary Papers*, 1927, vol. 26, 388–9 (*A Selection of Papers dealing with the relations between His Majesty's Government and the Soviet Government 1921–1927*: Cmnd. 2895). In this text MacDonald is shown as signing the letter. When it was issued it was signed J. D. Gregory. MacDonald pointed out the error at the time of publication in 1927.

5. Moreover, in the treaty which His Majesty's Government recently concluded with your Government, still further provision was made for the faithful execution of an analogous undertaking, which is essential to the existence of good and friendly relations between the two countries. His Majesty's Government means that these undertakings shall be carried out both in the letter and in the spirit, and it cannot accept the contention that whilst the Soviet Government undertakes obligations, a political body, as powerful as itself, is to be allowed to conduct a propaganda and support it with money, which is in direct violation with the official agreement. The Soviet Government either has or has not the power to make such agreements. If it has the power, it is its duty to carry them out and see that the other parties are not deceived. If it has not this power, and if responsibilities which belong to the State in other countries are in Russia in the keeping of private and irresponsible bodies, the Soviet Government ought not to make agreements which it knows it cannot carry out.

6. I should be obliged if you would be good enough to let me have the observations of your Government on this subject without delay.

I have, &c.

J. RAMSAY MACDONALD.

Index

Index

Memoirs, 108–32

Medical, Military Series, *History of the Second World War*, 186n.

Minutes of Evidence, 27, 29, 33–4, 37–40

Monthly journals, 160, 188n.

Monthly Digest of Statistics, 24

Morel (E. D.) papers, 81

Murray (Gilbert) papers, 80

Munitions, Ministry of, 69, 98, 185

Museums, 175–7

Museums and Galleries (Index publication), 177n.

National Buildings Record, 172

National Film Archive, 165–7

National Income and Expenditure, 183n.

National Income Statistics, 183

National Maritime Museum, 81

National Monuments Record, 172

National Museum of Wales, 176

National Physical Laboratory, 189n.

National Portrait Gallery, 171–2

National Register of Archives, 79, 165, 167

Nationalisation, 27, 29, 31, 69, 185n., 186n.

New Cambridge Modern History, 16n., 184n.

Newspapers, 24–5, 107, 109, 154–60, 199–209

Non-command papers, 27–8

Non-documentary sources, 163–78

Novels, 146–50

Nuffield College, 79, 81, 173

Occupations, 24, 50–1

Official history, 18, 43–4, 172, 184–7, 194

Official Secrets, 68, 78, 187

Parliamentary Debates (Hansard), 53–9, 105, 109, 154, 202, 206

Parliamentary Papers, 27–30 and n., 35, 42, 69, 218

Photographs, pictures, 170–2, 177

Plays, 152

Poetry, 150–2

Political and Economic Planning (P.E.P.), 139

Political memoirs, 115–25

Popular art, 152

Private members' bills, 55

Private papers, 77–82

Public Building and Works, 77n.

Public General Acts, 59

Public opinion polls, 143–4

Public Record Office, 63, 65–7, 75, 77

Public Records Acts, 63, 64

Public Schools Commission, 41

Quarterly publications, 160, 188n.

Radar, 190–1

Radio Times Hulton Picture Library, 171

Radio Research Laboratory, Slough, 190

Railway museums, 176

Record Repositories in Great Britain (H.M.S.O.), 81

Records of the Cabinet Office to 1922 (P.R.O.), 65n., 66–7

Reference works (standard), 23–6

Registrar-General's reports, 51–2

Registrar-General's Statistical Review of England and Wales, 51 and n., 52

Reviewers, 86, 107, 108, 110, 186–7

Robbins Report (education), 41

Royal Archives, Windsor, 65, 79, 92

Royal Commissions, 27, 28

Royal Institute of International Affairs, 26

Royal Services Institute Journal, 184n.

Royal Statistical Society Journal, 183n.

Russell papers, 80

Sample Census, 50

Samuel (Sir Herbert) report, 31, 32